LAW OF THE LAND

A Practical Legal Guide for Tourists and Business Travelers

France

By Michael L. Moore Esq.

Edited by Ally Knez-Siddique

Cover Design: Kristina Conatser

Published by: Law of the Land Publishing LLC

ISBN: 978-1-964870-06-9

DEDICATION

DEDICATION:

This book is dedicated to the memory of my late older brother, Kenneth Lee Moore, whose tragic murder at 15 years of age inspired me to write this series of books.

This book is also dedicated to my parents, John Henry Moore, and Edna Mae Moore, whose tremendous parenting skills kept me focused on the important things in life: being reverent, getting educated, and prioritizing family.

Finally, this book is dedicated to my beautiful family, my wife Royellen, my son AJ, and my daughter Karla. They inspire me every single day to be kind, patient, and compassionate.

IN LOVING MEMORY OF:

Belinda Joyce Moore Moss-my beautiful and wonderful sister, who supported me in every positive thing that I ever attempted to do.

Michael Eugene Baker-my dedicated and loyal friend and brother who always wanted the very best for me.

Sylvia Joyce Hill—my eldest sister, who had a beautiful spirit and was like a second mother to me.

LAW OF THE LAND®

PUBLISHING for Tourists & Business Travelers

Travel smart. Stay legal. Stay safe.®

From local laws to medical guides we've got you covered world wide **in one digital platform.**

Travel Safe Anywhere
3 MONTHS FREE TRIAL

SCAN QR code
for more info

PREFACE

My introduction to the justice system came when I was only 10 years old. My 15-year-old brother was murdered with a butcher knife by a 19-year-old in a simple argument over a torn shirt. I was devastated by his death and sought retribution for his fate that never came. The woman was initially charged with second degree murder, but after plea negotiations, she was convicted of manslaughter and sentenced to only five years in a youthful offender school and ordered to undergo psychiatric care. That was it. Nothing more. The judicial system had run its course.

My family knew nothing about the justice system, and we did not have the tools to advocate for ourselves. No one provided us with a written source to reference for guidance through this process. There was no easily accessible, easy to understand, definitive source to educate ourselves about the legal system that we suddenly and unexpectedly found ourselves immersed in after being victimized by such a violent criminal act.

As I got older, finished college, law school, and ultimately started practicing law, it became clear to me that most people are not knowledgeable about the law or how the judicial process works. If most people are uninformed here in the United States regarding the law and the legal process, how would they fare when in other countries? I realized that tourists and businesspeople who travel internationally needed access to information on how to navigate the legal system in other countries!

For many years, there has been considerable media attention focused on international travelers experiencing legal difficulties while traveling abroad. Most of these news stories gained attention in the United States and abroad because they involved American citizens facing punishment that was considered "unconventional" and "harsh" by United States' legal standards. I recall a news story in 1994 regarding Michael Fay, a young American male, who had broken the law in Singapore. He was convicted and sentenced to be caned and or whipped publicly. While the United States Government weighed in on the inappropriate and cruel nature of the punishment, the young American was beaten because he had been convicted under Singapore law.

Similarly, in recent years, international news stories have garnered headlines regarding foreign travelers and their issues with the laws of countries that were not their own. Amanda Knox, an American woman, was accused of murdering her roommate in Italy in 2007 and spent almost four years in an Italian prison before being definitively acquitted by the Supreme Court of Cassatio. Kenneth Bae, an American citizen, was arrested in North Korea in 2012 and was convicted for hostile acts against the communist country. He was sentenced to 15 years hard labor but was released in 2014 after efforts by the U.S. State Department. More recently, United States Basketball Star, Brittany Griner was arrested in February 2022 at a Moscow airport on drug-related charges and detained for nearly 10 months, spending much of that time in prison. Her plight unfolded at the same time Russia invaded Ukraine and further heightened tensions between Russia and the United States, ending only after she was freed in exchange for a notorious Russian arms dealer.

It was in 1994 that another personal tragic event occurred that finally inspired me to write these series of books. A dear friend and also client of mine was brutally murdered while on his second honeymoon in Jamaica. News of his murder shocked me and our local community. The legal hurdles his family had to overcome to see that justice was properly dispensed far away from home, in another country, with an entirely different set of criminal procedural rules and laws, was difficult to navigate.

As I was my friend's attorney at the time of his death, his family asked that I act as their "legal liaison" to the Jamaican Prosecutor's Office and to the Jamaican Police Department. I participated in multiple police interviews with my client's widow because she was the primary witness to his murder. As a former prosecuting attorney, I was also allowed by the Court, as a professional courtesy, to sit at the prosecutor's table to consult with the prosecuting attorney during trial. What I observed about the Jamaican trial process from a front row seat was compelling enough to cause me to seriously consider educating the "world" regarding what to expect and how to act appropriately when faced with legal issues while traveling abroad.

One of the realities in life is that, regardless of what country you are in, it is never a pleasant experience to run afoul of the law and be forced to accept that someone else will be making a decision about your pecuniary, proprietary, or penal interests (your money, your property, or your freedom).

It is important to know what the laws are, how they apply to you, and how to navigate the legal system if you are charged with a crime. It is also very helpful to know what resources are available to you if you are the victim of a criminal act. At the end of the day, an "ounce of prevention is worth a pound of cure," so the more knowledge you have, the more ammunition you possess, and the more likely you will have a positive outcome.

If you are traveling to France, the first thing you should pack is a copy of this book! The helpful information and tips contained in this volume will provide a great starting point for knowing what to do (and not to do!) when you arrive at your destination and will help ensure you have a wonderful vacation or business trip unmarred by tangles with the law.

TABLE OF CONTENTS

INTRODUCTION

INTRODUCTION

As a practicing attorney for over 34 years, I have encountered numerous clients who travel often but are unaware of the laws of the land they are traveling to.

Therefore, many years ago, I decided to write a series of books that would explain the laws of specific countries. My focus was to explain the laws that may affect travelers in a straightforward manner, without all of the legal language that is sometimes hard for even seasoned attorneys to understand.

About This Book

The aim of this book is simple. It provides you, the traveler, with a simple, easy to read book that will provide a basic legal guide that explains the law in the country that you are about to visit. It is not intended to educate you on ALL of the laws in a given country. The goal is to provide you with the details of the most common legal and safety issues faced by tourists and business travelers.

I have also provided context with background information on places not to visit, statistics on the country and prevention measures you should take to safeguard your legal and physical safety. Knowledge is a powerful thing and knowing how to stay out of trouble (or how to get out of it!) is important for everyone who travels.

This *Law of The Land/France* book simply helps you become more informed about your legal rights, responsibilities, and obligations in a wide range of subject areas.

Last, but not least, this book does NOT purport to offer legal advice. It does, however, provide the information you need to stay safe, follow the law and navigate around legal difficulties. However, if you do face legal difficulties, the information in this book will provide you with a starting point for solving the problem and obtaining legal assistance should it be required.

Hypotheticals Used Throughout This Book

From time to time throughout this book, I will explain the law to readers by using hypothetical scenarios. These hypotheticals will be marked by an icon that will be explained in further detail as you read on.

How This Book is Organized

CHAPTER 1: **About France.** This chapter will provide you with a brief overview about France and its history. It also addresses Visa requirements, monetary advice, and the best times to visit.

CHAPTER 2: **Customs.** This chapter will provide information on what to expect when entering France. It will also explain what restricted and prohibited items are when entering France along with customs regulations.

CHAPTER 3: **Crime in France.** This chapter provides an overview of the history of crime in France and steps French officials have taken to curb the high rate of crime.

CHAPTER 4: **Criminal Law Violations.** This chapter will provide information on drug offenses, penalties, true events and questions and answers.

CHAPTER 5: **Alcohol-Related Offenses.** This chapter will provide key points regarding the sale, consumption, and regulations of alcohol use in France.

CHAPTER 6: **Firearm & Ammunition Offenses.** This chapter will provide key points regarding the possession of firearms and ammunition in France.

CHAPTER 7: **Prostitution.** This chapter provides an overview of the history of prostitution in France, laws and penalties, prostitution practices, sex trafficking, sex tourism, health in France, tips to avoid being hassled, a Law of the Land Hypothetical and the current situation on prostitution in France.

CHAPTER 8: **LGBTQ.** This chapter will provide information regarding the acceptance of LGBTQ people in France and the laws surrounding homosexuality.

CHAPTER 9: **Sexually Motivated/Violent Crimes.** This chapter will provide an overview of sexually related crimes in France.

CHAPTER 10: **Arrested in France.** This chapter will provide information on what to do if you are arrested in France.

CHAPTER 11: **Jails vs. Prisons: Conditions & Culture.** This chapter will provide information on the conditions and culture of French Jails and Prisons.

CHAPTER 12: **Helping a Friend or Relative Imprisoned in France.** This chapter will provide information on how you can assist a friend or relative imprisoned in France.

CHAPTER 13: **The Administration of Justice.** This chapter will provide information on France's Judicial System.

CHAPTER 14: **Crime Victim Assistance.** This chapter will provide information on crime victim assistance along with providing safety tips.

CHAPTER 15: **Police.** This chapter will provide information on the French Police and how to report a crime.

CHAPTER 16: **How to Get Legal Help in France.** This chapter will provide information regarding how to obtain legal assistance for travelers to France.

CHAPTER 17: **Medical Facilities & Hospitals.** This chapter will provide information about how to obtain medical care while visiting France.

CHAPTER 18: **Driving in France.** This chapter will provide information on Driving in France, Traffic Rules, and Road Safety Tips.

CHAPTER 19: **Nude Beaches & Clothing-Optional Resorts.** This chapter will provide an overview of Nude beaches in France, and the legality and safety of visiting Nude beaches in France.

CHAPTER 20: **Unusual Laws.** This chapter will provide information on some Unusual Laws in France, and penalties and fines.

CHAPTER 21: **Traveling Safely.** This chapter will provide information on women traveling alone, crime prevention for families, safety notes for all travelers, and overall advice.

CHAPTER 22: **Tourist Taxation.** This chapter will provide information on taxes that tourists are required to pay in France.

CHAPTER 23: **Long-Term Stays.** This chapter will provide an overview of the consequences for overstaying your visit to France.

CHAPTER 24: **Civil Litigation.** This chapter will provide information about the civil litigation process in France.

CHAPTER 25: **Other Things to Know.** This chapter will provide information on the harassment of tourists, travel and safety, and other practical tips.

CHAPTER 26: **Quick Reference Guide.** This chapter is a quick way to get information. It is a condensed version of the chapters in this book.

Emergency/Important Contact Numbers in France

Useful French Phrases

Glossary

Icons Used in this Book

What do those pictures throughout the book mean? See below:

 **WARNING:** This icon flags information about things you should **avoid** while visiting France. Heed the advice next to this icon to avoid legal perils.

 **REMEMBER:** This icon flags noteworthy information that you shouldn't forget.

 **HELPFUL TIPS:** This icon flags information that will help you when entering France, relates to a legal situation, or refers to resources available while visiting France.

 **TECHNICAL INFORMATION:** This icon flags technical aspects of the law. If you are faced with a legal problem, and you want to learn more about the law involved, this information can be helpful.

 **ADDITIONAL INFORMATION**: This icon points to the location of additional information available on the internet.

 **HYPOTHETICAL**: This icon points to hypothetical scenarios to illustrate possible legal problems and the outcome.

 **QUESTIONS**: This icon points to questions and answers throughout the book.

 **TRUE STORY**: This icon points to true events throughout the book.

Where to Go From Here

If you have a specific question about the law in France as it relates to a particular area, just turn to the chapter that addresses that issue, or turn to the Quick Reference Guide.

You can also read the book from cover to cover to obtain a more comprehensive understanding of the French laws, and resources available should you find yourself in a legal predicament while visiting.

 **Disclaimer:** While the recommendations in this book primarily address U.S. citizens, the information is relevant and applicable to citizens of any country.

ABOUT FRANCE

IN THIS CHAPTER

- About France
- France, the Basics
- France's Hospitality
- General Questions
- Law of the Land True Story

CHAPTER 1
ABOUT FRANCE

About France

With a surface area of 547,030 km², or 211,209 miles², France is twice the size of the UK, and slightly smaller than the state of Texas. It is the biggest nation in Western Europe and borders Belgium, Luxembourg, Germany, Switzerland, France, Spain, and Andorra.[1]

France holds a deeply significant place in European history, shaped by key events and transformative movements. As the birthplace of the Enlightenment, it played a crucial role in shaping modern philosophical and political thought, influencing revolutions and democratic ideals across the globe. The French Revolution (1789-1799) had a profound impact on European history, giving rise to Napoleon Bonaparte and spreading revolutionary ideals throughout the continent. France also played pivotal roles in both World Wars, with historic battles such as the Battle of Verdun and the D-Day landings in Normandy being central to the Allied victory in World War II.

In terms of tourism, France is unrivaled as the world's most-visited country. Its rich cultural heritage, renowned cuisine, and vibrant arts scene make it a top destination for travelers seeking both historical and contemporary experiences. This combination of history and tourism solidifies France's importance in Europe. Geographically, it serves

---

1   https://about-france.com/in-brief.htm#brief

as a bridge between Northern and Southern Europe, bordered by the Atlantic Ocean, the Mediterranean Sea, the Alps, and the Pyrenees. France is Europe's leading agricultural producer and one of the world's major industrial powers.

France consistently ranks as the most-visited country in the world, according to the *United Nations World Tourism Organization*, with Paris being the third most-visited city globally. In 2018, France welcomed 89.4 million tourists, and in 2019, that number reached 90 million, drawn by its natural and architectural beauty and celebrated hospitality. Tourism represents nearly 10% of France's GDP.

Popular destinations include cities like Paris, Marseille, Nice, and Normandy, as well as regions such as the Loire Valley and Bordeaux. Major tourist attractions include the Eiffel Tower, Château de Versailles, Mont Saint-Michel, Arc de Triomphe, and Musée Picasso, along with the stunning French Riviera and the majestic French Alps. With its diverse landscapes—from vineyards and historic châteaux to the Mediterranean coastline and mountain peaks—France offers a wealth of experiences for visitors.

French People and Language

France stands as one of the most populous countries in Europe, with an estimated population of approximately 64.88 million people as of 2024. This population is characterized by its diversity, consisting of various ethnic groups, cultures, and religions that contribute to the nation's rich social fabric.[2]

French is the official language of France and is spoken by the vast majority of the population, approximately 87%. French serves not only as a means of communication but also as a significant cultural identifier, showcasing the nation's literary and artistic heritage. Additionally, various regional languages, such as Alsatian, Breton, and Occitan, are spoken

---

2   https://www.worldometers.info/world-population/
     france-population/#google_vignette

in certain areas, although they lack official recognition.[3] Furthermore, due to immigration, languages such as Arabic, Portuguese, and Spanish also reflect the linguistic diversity present in France today, highlighting the complex demographic landscape that characterizes the country.

Religion

Religion in France is diverse, with Christianity being the predominant faith, largely represented by Catholicism, which makes up roughly 50% of the population.[4] The country adheres to a strict principle of secularism (*laïcité*), which separates religion from government affairs and promotes freedom of thought and belief. Islam is recognized as the second-largest religion, followed by smaller communities of Jews, Protestants, and other faiths, contributing to the multicultural tapestry of French society. Notably, a significant portion of the population identifies as nonreligious or atheist, reflecting a growing trend toward secularism and individual belief systems in contemporary France.

Affordability

France presents a mixed picture of affordability for visitors, highly dependent on location and individual preferences. Major cities like Paris have high accommodation costs, with mid-range hotel prices ranging from €90 (US$93.63) to €190 (US$197.66) per night, while smaller towns offer more affordable options starting at around €60 (US$62.42). Transportation is manageable, with affordable public transport options, as a one-way metro ticket in Paris costs about €1.80 (US$1.87). Dining also varies widely, with budget-conscious travelers able to find meals for under €20 (US$20.81) or opt for grocery shopping and street food to save on costs. Entry fees for popular attractions range from free to about €20 (US$20.81), and discount passes are available for additional savings. Therefore, with strategic planning and smart choices, visitors can enjoy the beauty and culture of France without overspending.

---

3   https://www.bbc.co.uk/languages/european_languages/countries/france. shtml

4   https://en.wikipedia.org/wiki/Secularism_in_France

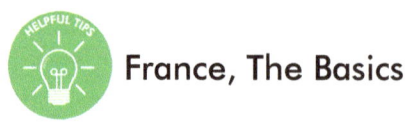

France, The Basics

How to Get There

Flying

France's major airports include **Charles de Gaulle** (CDG) near Paris, the largest and busiest, serving as a key international hub. **Orly Airport** (ORY), also near Paris, handles many domestic and short-haul flights. **Nice Côte d'Azur Airport** (NCE) serves the French Riviera, while **Lyon-Saint Exupéry Airport** (LYS) is a crucial hub in southeastern France. **Marseille Provence Airport** (MRS) supports the Provence region, and **Toulouse-Blagnac Airport** (TLS) is vital for the aerospace industry in Toulouse. **Bordeaux-Mérignac Airport** (BOD) serves Bordeaux and the Nouvelle-Aquitaine region. These airports are essential for both international and domestic travel.

By Train

Train transportation in and out of France is highly efficient and extensive, with the SNCF operating a vast network of high-speed TGV trains connecting major cities domestically and internationally. The **Eurostar** links Paris with London via the Channel Tunnel, while **Thalys** connects France with Belgium, the Netherlands, and Germany. Other significant international routes include TGV **Lyria** to Switzerland, and **RENFE-SNCF** to Spain. Domestically, TGV, Intercités, and regional TER trains provide comprehensive coverage, ensuring seamless travel across the country. French trains are known for their punctuality, comfort, and convenience, making rail a popular choice for travelers.

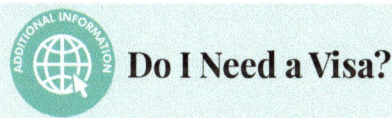

Do I Need a Visa?

Whether you need a visa to visit France depends on your nationality and the purpose of your visit. Citizens of the European Union, European Economic Area, and Switzerland do not need a visa for any length of stay. For short stays (up to 90 days within a 180-day period), citizens of many countries, including the USA, Canada, Australia, and Japan, do not need a visa for tourism or business. However, travelers from other countries or those planning to stay longer, or for purposes like work or study, will need to obtain a visa. Always check the latest requirements from the French consulate or embassy before traveling.

When Do I Visit?

The best time to visit France depends on your interests and the experiences you seek. **Spring** *(April to June)* is ideal for pleasant weather and blooming landscapes. It's perfect for exploring Paris, Provence's lavender fields, and the French Riviera before the summer crowds arrive.

Summer *(July to August)* is peak tourist season, especially along the coasts and in Paris. The weather is warm, festivals abound, and it's a great time for beach holidays in places like Nice or Biarritz. However, popular tourist spots can be crowded and more expensive.

Autumn *(September to November)* offers cooler temperatures, fewer tourists, and stunning fall foliage. This is an excellent time for wine enthusiasts to visit regions like Bordeaux and Burgundy during the grape harvest.

Winter *(December to March)* is perfect for skiing in the Alps or Pyrenees. Christmas markets in cities like Strasbourg and Colmar add festive charm. Paris and other cities have a quieter, more local feel, with cultural attractions less crowded.

Monetary Advice

The official currency is the euro. It's advisable to exchange some money before leaving home, as banks typically offer better rates than airport exchange services, which often have higher fees. Upon arrival, using ATMs (distributeurs automatiques de billets) is a convenient option, as they are widely available and generally provide favorable exchange rates. To avoid high fees, it's best to use ATMs associated with reputable banks.

Credit and debit cards, particularly Visa and MasterCard, are widely accepted in France. However, it's crucial to inform your bank of your travel plans to prevent your card from being blocked due to suspicious activity. Additionally, be aware of potential foreign transaction fees your bank might charge. If possible, consider obtaining a credit card that doesn't charge such fees.

While cards are convenient, it's wise to carry some cash for smaller establishments, markets, and tips, as not all places accept cards. Monitoring exchange rates through apps or websites can help ensure you get a fair deal when exchanging money. In large cities like Paris, more and more establishments are going cashless so make sure you have a credit or debit card available. Please be aware of potential international fees.

Tipping and Bargaining

In France, tipping is generally not obligatory due to a service charge of approximately 15% being included in restaurant bills, indicated by "*service compris*." While leaving gratuity is appreciated for exceptional service, it typically involves rounding up the bill or leaving a few euros. In other service sectors, such as hotels and taxis, tipping is also not required, but small gestures of appreciation are common, reflecting the country's values of respect and social equality.

Bargaining is generally expected in flea markets and antique shops in France, where vendors anticipate negotiations over prices, with customers typically starting their offers 20-30% lower than the asking price. In contrast, fixed-price retail settings, including boutiques and food markets, do not permit haggling, as prices are set and regulated.

French Hospitality

French hospitality is renowned for its elegance, reflecting the country's cultural traditions and the concept of *"art de vivre"*—the art of living well. Guests are treated with great respect, often enjoying multi-course meals made from fresh, local ingredients, paired with fine wines. In both private homes and the hospitality industry, exceptional service is a hallmark, with attentive hosts creating a welcoming environment. Rural bed-and-breakfasts, or *"chambres d'hôtes,"* offer an intimate experience, where guests often share meals and stories with their hosts, adding a personal touch to their stay.

In French culture, greetings and formalities play a vital role, with *"Bonjour"* expected in social interactions and the use of titles such as *Madame* or *Monsieur* deemed respectful. Dining etiquette requires waiting for the host to start the meal, maintaining proper table manners, and finishing all food on one's plate to demonstrate appreciation. Conversationally, discussions of personal topics such as income or political beliefs are typically viewed as impolite, while using formal address and allowing others to speak without interruption reflects courtesy.

General Questions

1. *Must I present any documents, other than my passport, when I get to the border control in the Schengen area?* **Yes**, in addition to your passport, you may be required to present supporting documents at border control in the Schengen area. These may include proof of the purpose of your trip, evidence of sufficient funds for your stay, and a certificate of travel insurance covering medical expenses, hospitalization, and repatriation. If you hold a visa, it must be valid, and border police may also ask for evidence of your means to return to your home country.

2. *I ran out of time to complete my visa application before my departure, can I ask for a visa when I arrive in France?* No. France authorities don't issue visa at your arrival. Unless exempt from having a visa, you must have a visa issued before your arrival in France or within the Schengen area. As a reminder, having a visa in your passport does not necessarily guarantee the holder will be authorized to enter the Schengen area, and the border police may refuse your entry.

3. *How to calculate the travel days remaining on my Schengen short-stay visa?* For the Schengen short-stay visa, the European Commission website has created a calculator, that can help you check how many days are left on your visa (Reminder: the total length of your stay must not exceed a total of 90 days over a period of 180 days). You can find the calculator at the following link:

 **https://ec.europa.eu/assets/home/visa-calculator/calculator.htm?lang=fr**

Law of the Land True Story

Mehran Karimi Nasseri, an Iranian refugee, famously lived in Terminal 1 of Paris's Charles de Gaulle Airport from 1988 to 2006. He had arrived in France without proper documentation and found himself trapped in a bureaucratic limbo, unable to leave the airport due to lack of ID papers or a passport, yet unable to board a plane to return home. This unique situation, which became a symbol of statelessness, lasted for 18 years. Ultimately, health issues, exacerbated by the polluted airport environment, led to his relocation to a homeless shelter in Paris, marking the end of his extraordinary airport stay.

CHAPTER 2

CUSTOMS

CUSTOMS

 **Travelers Entering France**

All passengers arriving in France are required to present their passport, along with the completed Customs form to a Customs Officer for processing. You should respond truthfully to all questions and accurately declare what is in your possession. This includes a requirement to report any food, plants, animal products, and monetary instruments.

Upon arrival at the port of entry, passengers must go through several procedures. First, at passport control, EU/EEA citizens can use automated gates, while non-EU travelers undergo manual checks. Next, passengers may need to declare items exceeding duty-free limits, such as cash over €10,000 or commercial goods. After collecting baggage from the designated carousel, travelers proceed to customs, where they may undergo a random inspection or be asked to declare specific items.

Customs Entitlements

Entering France

When entering France, travelers must declare any cash equivalent to €10,000 (US$10,403) or more, as failure to do so may result in confiscation or fines.[5] Additionally, certain goods are prohibited, including illegal drugs, counterfeit items, and specific plants and animals, which are subject to strict regulatory controls. Furthermore, restrictions apply to importing food products from non-EU countries, particularly concerning animal origin items, requiring compliance with sanitary and phytosanitary certificates to ensure they meet health standards. For a list of prohibited items, refer to:

 **https://www.service-public.fr/particuliers/vosdroits/ F3161?lang=en.**

Exiting France

When returning from France, you must declare if you're carrying €10,000 (US$10,403) or more in cash or monetary instruments, filling out a declaration form for customs. Failure to declare this amount can result in fines or confiscation. You can bring back items like wine, spirits, cheese, perfume, fashion items, and gourmet foods within specific limits, but be cautious with food, especially dairy and meat, as regulations vary by country. Always check your home country's customs rules before traveling.

---

5   https://europa.eu/youreurope/citizens/travel/carry/carrying-cash/ index_en.htm

 **Money and Monetary Instruments**

Passengers can bring money and monetary instruments into or out of France, but there are specific rules to follow. If you are carrying €10,000 (or its equivalent in other currencies, including US$10,000) or more, you must declare it to French customs. Here are the steps to take:

1. **Fill Out a Declaration Form:** Obtain the declaration form from customs or download it from the French customs website. This form requires you to provide details about the amount of money, its origin, and its intended use.

2. **Submit the Declaration:** Present the completed form to a customs officer upon arrival. This can typically be done at the customs office in the airport or border crossing point.

3. **Prepare for Inspection:** Be ready for customs officers to inspect the cash or monetary instruments you are carrying.

Failing to declare amounts over €10,000 (US$10,403) can result in the money being confiscated and possible legal penalties. Always ensure to comply with customs regulations to avoid issues.[6]

 Failure to comply with these requirements will result in a breach of France's customs regulations, subject to fines and penalties.[7]

---

6   https://franceintheus.org/IMG/pdf/trouble_free_travel_with_french_customs-2.pdf

7   https://www.service-public.fr/particuliers/vosdroits/F3161?lang=en

Restricted and Prohibited Items

When traveling to France, be aware of restricted and prohibited items. Prohibited items include illegal drugs, unauthorized weapons and ammunition, counterfeit goods, items made from endangered species (like ivory), and pornographic material.

Restricted items have specific limits and conditions. For **alcohol**, you can bring up to 4 liters of still wine, 16 liters of beer, 1 liter of spirits over 22% alcohol, or 2 liters of fortified wine or liqueurs. For **tobacco**, limits include 200 cigarettes, 100 cigarillos, 50 cigars, or 250 grams of tobacco. **Personal use medicines** should be accompanied by a prescription, and some may need special permits. **Certain food items**, particularly meat, dairy, and plant products, may be restricted to prevent disease spread. **Cultural artifacts** might need special permits for import. Additionally, **cash** amounts over €10,000 (or equivalent to US$10,403) must be declared upon entry and exit.[8]

Five Practical Tips to Know Before You Go

Before traveling to France, it's essential to understand a few key points for a smooth and enjoyable trip:

1. Politeness is highly valued so make sure to respect local customs.

2. Ensure you have travel insurance that covers health expenses, and EU citizens should carry a European Health Insurance Card (EHIC). In case of emergencies, dial 112.

3. Additionally, France uses a 230V supply voltage and 50Hz, with type C and E plugs, so bring appropriate adapters if needed.

4. Note that many shops are closed on Sundays and may have shorter hours on Mondays.

---

8   https://www.trade.gov/country-commercial-guides/
    france-customs-regulations

5. Ensure your passport is valid for at least three months beyond your planned departure date from the Schengen area, and check visa requirements if applicable.

 **General Questions**

1. *Do I need a visa to travel to France?* It depends on your nationality. Citizens of the EU, US, Canada, and several other countries do not need a visa for short stays (up to 90 days). Check with the French consulate or embassy for specific requirements based on your citizenship.

2. *Are there any health precautions I should take?* Ensure you have travel insurance with health coverage. The European Health Insurance Card (EHIC) is useful for EU travelers. Check if any vaccinations are recommended based on your travel itinerary.

3. *What are the emergency contact numbers in France?* The emergency number in France is **112** for police, fire, and medical emergencies.

4. *What should I know about French customs regulations?* You can bring certain quantities of alcohol and tobacco without customs duties. Be aware of restrictions on bringing in certain food items and declare if carrying €10,000 (US$10,403) or more.

5. *Should I pay custom dues for money and other monetary-equivalent instruments I bring into France?* When bringing money or monetary-equivalent instruments into France, you generally do not have to pay customs duties. However, you must declare amounts of €10,000 (US$10,403 or its equivalent in other currencies) or more when entering or leaving France. This applies to cash, traveler's checks, and other forms of monetary instruments.

6. *Are there tax-free/duty-free stores in France that tourists can take advantage of while visiting?* In France, tourists can enjoy tax-free shopping for goods purchased at participating stores. To qualify, non-EU residents must spend a minimum amount (typically around €100.01 or US$104.04) and obtain a tax refund form. The form must be validated at the airport or customs office before departure. Additionally, duty-free shopping is available at airports and ports for travelers leaving the EU, with limits on items like alcohol and tobacco. Ensure you follow the regulations for both tax-free and duty-free shopping to benefit from these options.

 ## Law of the Land Hypothetical

If you received a US$700 bracelet as a gift and bought a US$40 hat and a US$60 print, totaling US$800, you would not be charged duty, as you haven't exceeded your duty-free exemption. However, if you also bought a US$500 painting, you could bring the entire US$1,300 worth of merchandise home without paying duty, because fine art is duty-free.

CHAPTER 3

CRIME IN FRANCE

CHAPTER 3

CRIME IN FRANCE

Overview[9]

Paris has a moderate crime risk but is generally considered safe for tourists, students, and business travelers. Cities like Bordeaux, Lyon, Marseille, Rennes, Strasbourg, and Toulouse have minimal crime risks. While violent crimes are rare, street crime is more of a concern, with tourists often falling victim to opportunistic theft. Theft, including pickpocketing, bag snatching, and house burglaries, is common, particularly in major cities and popular tourist spots like the Louvre, the Eiffel Tower, and public transportation. Thieves often target smartphones, small electronics, and items of high value. As electronics, especially Apple products, can be more expensive in France compared to places like the U.S., it's important to be cautious where you store or use devices like smartphones and laptops.

Organized crime, including pickpocketing, is a significant concern in France, particularly in tourist-heavy areas like train stations, subways, and airports, where criminals use distraction tactics. For example, one thief might engage a tourist with questions while an accomplice steals their belongings. Many pickpockets in Paris are children under sixteen, as they are less likely to face legal consequences. To combat theft, the French government has increased police presence in high-risk areas,

---

9   https://www.osac.gov/Country/France/Content/Detail/ Report/555db84c-e977-430b-9379-15f4aeadf3a0

launched public awareness campaigns, and enhanced security at popular tourist sites. Tourists are advised to remain vigilant and protect their belongings.

Organized crime also fuels much of France's violent crimes, and tourists are often targeted by scams. One common scam involves criminals posing as legitimate companies to trick tourists into sending money for fake prizes or lottery winnings. It is crucial not to send money in response to such claims and to verify any offers through official channels.

Terrorism remains a concern in major cities, including Paris, Bordeaux, Lyon, Marseille, Rennes, Strasbourg, and Toulouse, primarily from foreign fighters. The French government is focused on counterterrorism, disrupting networks, preventing radicalization, and improving community resilience. While the threat persists, staying vigilant, reporting suspicious activities, and following safety guidelines are vital to ensuring a safe visit.

 In light of these safety concerns, visitors are urged to visit the United States Department of State's website, (or its equivalent in other countries), at **https://www.state.gov/**, for updates on the "safety status" for visiting France and adhering to recommended safety guidelines. This includes being aware of one's surroundings, practicing discretion with valuables and avoiding risky areas, especially during nighttime. While the allure of France's natural beauty and cultural richness is undeniable, travelers should approach their visit with a balanced perspective that considers both the positive aspects and the need for cautious exploration.

Crime Statistics

In 2023, France recorded 845 homicides, resulting in a homicide rate of approximately 1.25 per 100,000 people, according to official data published by the Ministry of the Interior. The United Nations considers any homicide rate of 10 per 100,000 citizens or above to be an "epidemic."

France's total killings in 2023 marked a slight increase from 2022's total of 830 but remained a significant improvement over 2017's sum of 900.[10]

Drug-related crimes are a significant issue, with substantial seizures made by law enforcement. Cybercrime has also been on the rise, with increasing reports of online fraud and identity theft. Rural areas generally report lower crime rates, with fewer violent crimes but occasional property crimes.

The government responded by increasing police presence and expanding the use of surveillance technologies, particularly in high-crime areas and in response to terrorist threats. Despite these efforts, public perception of safety varies, with many citizens expressing concerns about rising crime rates and varying levels of trust in law enforcement.

 For the most accurate and updated information, refer to official reports from the Ministry of the Interior at **https://www.interieur.gouv.fr/**

 ## Quick Safety Tips[11]

Here are some quick safety tips to help avoid becoming a victim in France:

- Carry only essential items and leave valuables like jewelry, extra cash, and your passport in the hotel safe.

---

10 https://sustainabledevelopment.un.org/content/documents/5987our-common-future.pdf

11 https://fr.usembassy.gov/services/lost-and-found-property-in-paris/safety-advice-for-paris/

- You don't need to carry your passport with you at all times; a student card or driver's license is usually sufficient for ID.

- Keep your purse or shoulder bag close in crowded places and avoid carrying valuables in easily accessible spots. Women should keep bags under their arm and away from the street.

- Be cautious around noisy groups of children in busy areas, as they are often skilled pickpockets.

- Never leave valuables in an unlocked car, even in the trunk.

- If mugged, do not resist; report the theft immediately to the nearest police station for a theft report, which is helpful for insurance claims. If your passport is stolen, inform your embassy.

General Questions

1. *What types of crimes are common in France?* Theft, including pickpocketing, bag snatching, burglaries, and muggings are common, especially in large cities like Paris. In February 2024, the most common type of crime reported to the police was nonviolent theft.

2. *Where is crime most prevalent in France?* Property crime is most prevalent in Paris and the Mediterranean coastal cities of Marseille and Nice. Muggings are common in the Ile de France region, which includes Paris and its outer suburbs.

3. *What are some safety tips for travelers in France?* Be especially vigilant with your safety and belongings at automated service stations, rest areas on motorways, and military cemeteries in Normandy. Always protect your PIN at ATMs, particularly in high-traffic tourist areas and automated service stations where pickpockets may be more active.

🔴 Law of the Land True Story

Four American tourists, two adults and two kids, boarded a crowded metro during rush hour, each carrying multiple bags as they traveled to a new Airbnb. While standing near the doors, they chatted in English about their stops. A couple of men had aggressively pushed their way onto the train, likely scouting for opportunities to pickpocket. At the next stop, one of the men pretended his shoe was stuck under a tourist's suitcase, prompting the man to lean over and assist. As he did, the other thief quickly swiped the tourist's wallet from his back pocket, and both thieves dashed out of the train doors, disappearing into the crowd before the tourist could react.

CHAPTER 4
CRIMINAL LAW VIOLATIONS

IN THIS CHAPTER

- Marijuana and Other Drugs in France
- Prescription Medication
- Penalties
- General Questions
- Law of the Land Hypothetical
- Takeaways

CHAPTER 4

CRIMINAL LAW VIOLATIONS

 Marijuana and Other Drugs in France

Compared to the rest of Europe, France has stricter regulations regarding marijuana use. While offenders once faced severe penalties, including fines of up to €3,750 (US$3,901.13) and up to one year in prison, regulations were revised in 2018. Under the new rules, fines for cannabis possession of small quantities for personal use were reduced to €150-200 (US$156.04 – $208.06). In September 2020, these fines were standardized to a fixed €200 (US$208.06), with the infraction recorded electronically by the police.[12]

An offender charged with personal use faces a maximum prison sentence of 1 year and a fine, although in minor cases prosecution may be waived or simplified. The maximum sentence increases if the offender endangered users of transport or if the offense was committed by a public servant while on duty. As with many crimes, sentences may be doubled in the event of a subsequent offense within a 5-year period.

---

12 https://www.interieur.gouv.fr/Le-ministre/Communiques-du-ministre/Generalisation-du-dispositif-d-amende-forfaitaire-delictuelle-pour-usage-de-stupefiants-au-1er-septembre-2020

In France, the laws governing illegal substances do not differentiate between drugs in terms of severity. However, it is up to the discretion of the judge to decide whether the person charged with a drug offense should be sent to a rehabilitation facility or face legal penalties.

Marijuana possession, usage, cultivation, and trafficking are prohibited and carry serious legal repercussions. The following are the key points about marijuana-related offenses:

- Both marijuana usage and possession are prohibited. First-time offenders may also be subject to further penalties in addition to a fine of up to €200 (US$208.06). More severe penalties, including incarceration, may be imposed for repeat violations or aggravating circumstances.[13]

- It is illegal to grow marijuana, even for personal use. Penalties according to the size and conditions of the cultivation may include up to 20 years in prison and significant fines.

- Marijuana distribution and trafficking are serious crimes. The most severe penalty is ten years in prison and a fine of up to €7.5 million (US$7,798,500). If there are any minors involved or the crimes happen close to schools, the penalties are higher.

Although it is still illegal to use marijuana recreationally, France has taken efforts to enable its medical usage. In 2021, a pilot program was launched to examine the provision of medical cannabis to specific individuals under stringent guidelines.

Operating a vehicle while under the influence of marijuana is forbidden. If it causes accidents or puts others in danger, it may result in fines, license suspension, or even jail time.[14]

---

13   https://www.loc.gov/item/global-legal-monitor/2020-09-23/
     france-possession-of-small-amounts-of-drugs-now-subject-to-fines/

14   https://www.europarl.europa.eu/RegData/etudes/BRIE/2023/749792/
     EPRS_BRI(2023)749792_EN.pdf

 ## Legal Status of Delta 8 in France

Delta 8 THC, a cannabinoid similar to the more commonly known Delta 9 THC, has sparked debate regarding its legality, especially in countries with strict cannabis regulations like France. While hemp cultivation for industrial and commercial purposes is legal in France, the THC content in hemp products must not exceed 0.2%. Since Delta 8 THC is synthesized from CBD, it occupies a legal gray area. It's important to note that this information is not a substitute for official legal advice but aims to provide general awareness on the issue.

While France's 0.3% THC threshold suggests Delta 8 THC may not be permitted, there are no specific regulations addressing it, leaving consumers and businesses uncertain. The French government has taken a conservative stance toward psychoactive cannabinoids, and legal guidelines are still evolving. Delta 8's legal ambiguity stems from its synthetic extraction from CBD, which complicates its alignment with natural THC content requirements. Given this nuanced legal situation, it's important to stay informed about potential changes to ensure compliance with the law.

 ## Other Drugs in France

French law prohibits the use, i.e. consumption, of controlled drugs. Around 200 psychoactive substances are banned and referred to sas "narcotics," among others cannabis, ecstasy, and cocaine. This prohibition applies to all consumption, whether individual or collective, private or public, occasional or repeated, with the sole exception of controlled substances contained in prescription medicines.

The French legal system also emphasizes treatment and rehabilitation for offenders, especially first-time and minor offenders. However, trafficking and distribution of illicit drugs carry much harsher penalties, reflecting the serious approach France takes toward combating drug-related crimes.

 ## Prescription Medication[15]

Article L 5111-1 of the French Public Health Code defines a medicinal product as "any substance or combination of substances presented as possessing curative or preventive properties with regard to human or animal diseases (medical product by presentation), and "any substance or combination of substances that may be used in or administered to humans or animals in order to make a medical diagnosis or to restore, correct or modify their physiological functions by exerting a pharmacological, immunological or metabolic action (medical product by function)."

When carrying medicinal products for personal use, the importation conditions are as follows:

Non-narcotic and non-psychotropic medicinal products:

- The quantity should correspond to the length of treatment prescribed or, if no prescription exists, treatment for up to three months.
- A doctor's prescription is required if the treatment exceeds three months.

Narcotic drugs or psychotropic substances:

- These can only be carried personally.
- The quantity should match the prescribed treatment or, if no prescription is available, treatment for up to one month under normal use conditions.

---

15 https://www.douane.gouv.fr/fiche/
  private-individuals-carrying-medicinal-products-france

Article 75 of the Schengen Agreement outlines the regulations for bringing medicinal products into a Schengen area country based on the country of origin.

From a Schengen Area Member State:

* The quantity transported must be compatible with personal therapeutic use.
* A certificate issued by the competent authorities of the country of origin is mandatory for customs.

For shipments to France:

* The individual must present the original prescription and a transport authorization issued by the regional health agency where the prescribing practitioner is registered.
* The transport authorization is valid for 30 days, within the duration of the prescribed treatment.

Penalties

French law does not distinguish between illicit substances and thus, an offense such as drug use is prosecuted and judged in the same way regardless of the illicit substance involved. However, judicial authorities may take into consideration the nature of the substance, the quantity and any prior criminal records in their decision to prosecute, reduce the charges, or not to prosecute an offender at all. Illicit substances are listed in an annex to Decree Law of 22 February 1990 and include the following:

* **List I:** narcotic substances such as heroin, cocaine, cannabis, methadone, opium, etc.;

- **List II:** substances such as codeine, propiram, etc.;

- **List III:** psychotropic substances such as amphetamines, ecstasy, LSD, etc.; and

- **List IV:** synthetic drugs such as MBDB, 4-MTA, ketamine, nabilone, THC, etc.[16]

The penalties for marijuana possession in France are strict, reflecting the country's stringent drug laws. As of 2023, here are the key points regarding marijuana possession:

Possession for Personal Use

- **First-Time Offenders:** A fixed fine of €200 (US$208.06) is typically issued for first-time offenders caught with small amounts of marijuana for personal use. If the fine is paid promptly, it may preclude further legal action.

- **Repeat Offenders:** Repeat offenses or larger quantities can lead to more severe penalties, including higher fines and potential imprisonment.

Possession with Intent to Distribute

- **Intent to Distribute:** Possessing marijuana with the intent to distribute or sell is a more serious offense, punishable by up to 10 years in prison and a fine of up to €7.5 million (US$7,798,500).

- **Aggravating Circumstances:** If the offense involves aggravating factors, such as selling to minors or within certain protected zones (near schools, for example), the penalties can be even harsher.

---

16 https://sencanada.ca/en/content/sen/committee/371/ille/library/ france-e#:~:text=The%20penalty%20for%20illicit%20drug,%2C%20 %22injonction%20th%C3%A9rapeutique%22

Cultivation and Trafficking

- **Cultivation:** Growing marijuana plants is illegal and can result in severe penalties, including imprisonment and substantial fines.
- **Trafficking:** Involvement in marijuana trafficking is treated very seriously, with penalties that can include long-term imprisonment and multimillion-dollar fines.

 **General Questions**

1. *Is cannabis legal in France?* Cannabis is illegal for recreational use in France. Possession, sale, and use can result in fines and imprisonment. However, France has a limited medical marijuana program, allowing certain patients with specific conditions to access cannabis-based medicines under strict regulation and prescription by a medical professional.

   Products containing cannabidiol (CBD), a non-psychoactive compound, are legal if they contain less than 0.2% THC, the psychoactive compound in cannabis. Industrial hemp cultivation is also legal, provided the THC content is below 0.2%. However, despite ongoing debates about drug policy reform, recreational cannabis remains illegal, with strict penalties enforced for violations.

2. *What are the penalties for possessing and consuming cannabis in France?* In France, possessing and consuming cannabis is illegal and subject to strict penalties. For first-time offenders, a fixed fine of €200 (US$207.96) is typically issued, and prompt payment can prevent further legal action. Repeat offenders face higher fines and the possibility of imprisonment.

Law of the Land Hypothetical

HYPOTHETICAL: *In France, Mario was arrested for possession of cocaine. He heard that in the past, judges have ordered lenient sentences for first-time offenders. Mario is hoping to obtain lenient sentences, since he is a first-time offender in France. Can Mario argue in court that precedence in prior cases dictates that he should receive a lenient sentence?*

ANSWER: **No.** *Mario cannot argue precedence in a French court, as France follows a civil law system. In this system, the focus is on written statutes and codes rather than case law. Unlike common law systems, where stare decisis (the principle of following previous court decisions) plays a significant role, civil law systems base decisions on the specific facts of each case and how they align with codified laws. Judges in France interpret and apply the law to each case individually, without being bound by prior rulings.*

Takeaways

- **Strict Laws:** Possession and trafficking of drugs are heavily penalized, with fines and prison sentences. Even small amounts of illegal drugs can result in severe consequences.

- **Penalties for Possession:** Possessing drugs can lead to fines up to €3,750 (US$3,899.25) and up to one year in prison.

- **Trafficking:** Drug trafficking carries severe penalties, ranging from five years to life in prison and heavy fines.

- **Cannabis:** While cannabis is illegal, penalties for small amounts of personal possession have been reduced to fines.

- **Public Use:** Using drugs in public places can lead to fines and arrest.

- **Delta-8 THC:** The legal status of cannabis derivatives like Delta-8 THC is unclear, but France remains conservative regarding psychoactive substances.

- **Foreign Nationals:** Foreigners are subject to the same drug laws as French citizens and face similar penalties.

- **Importing Drugs:** Importing drugs, including certain medicinal substances, is strictly controlled and requires proper documentation.

LAW OF THE LAND FRANCE

CHAPTER 5

ALCOHOL-RELATED OFFENSES

ALCOHOL-RELATED OFFENSES

Overview

France is well-known for its drinking culture, particularly for wine, which is deeply embedded in the country's history and daily life. Wine is often consumed with meals and is an important part of French social gatherings, with each region having its own distinct wine traditions. In addition to wine, France is famous for its sophisticated cocktail culture, champagne, and a variety of local spirits, making alcohol an integral part of the country's culinary and social landscape. However, alcohol-related offenses are taken seriously and are subject to strict regulations. These laws cover a range of behaviors, from public intoxication to driving under the influence. Understanding the legal consequences of alcohol-related offenses is crucial for both residents and visitors to ensure compliance and avoid penalties.

The legal drinking age in France is eighteen, and this rule is strictly enforced across the country, including in Paris. Establishments serving alcohol are required to verify proof of age, so always be prepared to show your identification, especially if you're near the legal drinking age. The same legal age applies throughout France, regardless of the region or city.[17]

---

17   https://secretsofparis.com/practical/health-safety/smoking-drinking/

In France, alcohol can be purchased in supermarkets, convenience stores, or wine boutiques, typically until 10 p.m. (or 8 p.m. in places where consumption is prohibited after 4). While there are no general open container laws, certain areas restrict public drinking after 4 p.m., including landmarks like the Champs-Elysées, Eiffel Tower, and Notre-Dame, as well as nightlife districts like the Latin Quarter and Canal Saint-Martin. Additionally, alcohol is not allowed in public parks, except in cafés within the parks.

Alcohol-Related Offenses

In France, alcohol- related offenses are taken seriously and can result in various legal consequences:

- **Driving Under the Influence (DUI):** The legal blood alcohol concentration (BAC) limit is 0.05% (0.02% for new drivers and professional drivers). Driving under the influence can lead to fines ranging from €135 to €4,500 (US$140.37 – $4,679.10), license suspension for up to 3 years, and imprisonment for up to 2 years. Severe cases, including repeat offenses or high BAC levels, can result in more severe penalties, including longer imprisonment and higher fines.

- **Public Intoxication:** Public intoxication is generally not a criminal offense but can lead to fines and detention if it results in disruptive behavior or endangers public safety. Fines can range from €38 to €150 (US$39.51 – 155.97), depending on the severity of the behavior.

- **Sales to Minors:** The legal drinking age in France is eighteen. This applies to purchasing and consuming alcoholic beverages in public and private settings. Selling alcohol to minors can result in fines and potential business license suspension for establishments that violate this law.

- **Alcohol-Related Violence:** Acts of violence or disturbances caused by alcohol consumption can lead to criminal charges. Depending on the severity, offenders may face fines, imprisonment, or both, along with additional legal consequences.

Alcohol Regulation

The *Évin Law*, formally established in 1991, serves as a cornerstone of alcohol regulation in France, addressing concerns related to public health and the influence of alcohol marketing. This law prohibits advertising alcoholic beverages on television and in cinemas, limiting promotional activities to the print media intended for adults.[18] Furthermore, the *Évin Law* stipulates that any alcohol advertising must provide factual information about the product without associating it with pleasure or success. For instance, advertisements cannot depict images that suggest glamour or youthfulness, focusing instead on the product's origin, composition, and means of production.

In France, the legal drinking age for bars and clubs is eighteen, and proof of age is required, though enforcement may not be as strict as in the U.S. Minors under sixteen can only enter establishments serving alcohol when accompanied by a parent. To protect young people, the *Évin Law* restricts alcohol sales at certain times and places, while also banning advertisements targeting minors and requiring health warnings. The government also runs public health campaigns to raise awareness about the risks of excessive drinking, particularly among teenagers and young adults.

Enforcement

The enforcement of alcohol regulations in France is executed primarily by two national police forces: the **Police Nationale** and the **Gendarmerie Nationale**. The Police Nationale operates mainly in urban areas, while the Gendarmerie Nationale serves rural communities, including smaller towns. These agencies are empowered to conduct checks in public venues such as bars, restaurants, and events where alcohol is served, ensuring adherence to regulations, including age restrictions and responsible

---

18   https://movendi.ngo/news/2020/06/19/
     france-alcohol-advertising-ban-wins-case-in-high-court

serving practices. Additionally, local law enforcement officers often collaborate with health inspectors to monitor compliance with the *Évin Law*.

Alcohol Allowances Entering and Exiting France

When traveling to and from France, it's important to adhere to customs regulations, particularly regarding alcohol allowances. These rules govern how much alcohol you can bring into the country, ensuring compliance with safety and legal standards. Travelers should familiarize themselves with the specific customs limits for alcohol to avoid penalties and ensure a smooth entry or exit.

Alcohol allowance when entering France from another EU Member State (no customs declaration required when traveling from another EU Member State). Please note that these allowances cannot be combined.[19]

Allowances for alcohol purchased in another EU Member State (no customs declaration required)

ALLOWANCES	TYPE OF GOODS
110 liters	Beer
+ 90 liters	Wine (including up to 60 litres of sparkling wine)
+ 20 liters	Intermediate products (e.g. vermouth, port wine, madeira wine)
+ 10 liters	Spirits (e.g. whisky, gin, vodka)

19 https://www.douane.gouv.fr/fiche/what-know-when-travelling-france

Alcohol allowance when entering France from a non-EU country (no customs declaration required when traveling from a non-EU country)

ALLOWANCES	TYPE OF GOODS
16 liters	Beer
4 liters	Still wine (non-sparkling)
2 liters	Intermediate products (e.g. vermouth, port wine, madeira wine)
OR 1 liter	Spirits (e.g. whisky, gin, vodka)
OR 1	Proportional assortment of the two previous categories

When exiting France, travelers must also adhere to specific regulations regarding the transportation of alcohol. The allowances primarily depend on the destination country. For travelers departing to another EU member state, the allowances echo those for entering, allowing individuals to carry significant quantities without specific limits, provided that it is for personal use.

In contrast, when traveling to non-EU countries, different restrictions may apply. Many non-EU countries impose their own customs regulations regarding the importation of alcohol, which travelers must adhere to upon arrival in their destination country. Therefore, it is advisable for travelers to research the alcohol importation laws of their destination to avoid any form of infringement.

General Questions

1. *Can a police officer detain you for drinking alcohol in a public place?* **Yes**, if you are intoxicated, you can be detained for 6 hours.

2. *Can a police officer fine you for drinking in a public place such as outside a bar or restaurant?* **Yes**, the fine is €150 (US$155.97), if you are intoxicated.

3. *As a tourist, can my driver's license be retained by the police if I a suspected of a DUI?* **Yes.** Your driver's license can be held up to 72 hours.

Law of the Land True Story

In 2012, French actor Gérard Depardieu was involved in a scooter accident in Paris, where a blood alcohol test revealed a level of 1.8, nearly three times the legal limit of 0.5. In 2013, he was found guilty of driving while intoxicated, resulting in a fine of €4,000 (US$4,159.20) and a six-month suspension of his driver's license.

FIREARM & AMMUNITION OFFENSES

IN THIS CHAPTER

- Current Firearm Status
- Traveling to France With a Firearm
- Penalties
- General Questions
- Law of the Land Hypothetical
- Takeaways

FIREARM & AMMUNITION OFFENSES

Current Firearm Status[20]

Gun ownership in France is a rigorously regulated matter that balances the rights of individuals to own firearms with the high priority placed on public safety. Through age restrictions, licensing requirements, comprehensive checks, and ongoing public health initiatives, France aims to maintain a safe environment while allowing responsible gun ownership. Here are the main points regarding gun ownership in France:

Legal Framework and Categorization: Firearms in France are classified into four categories based on their dangerousness, with Category A comprising prohibited weapons and Categories B and C involving more strictly regulated firearms.[21] This classification system dictates the requirements for ownership, usage, and transport.

Licensing Requirements: To own a firearm, individuals must obtain appropriate licenses, which include various conditions such as affiliation

---

20 https://www.connexionfrance.com/news/how-to-declare-possession-of-a-gun-in-france/131640#:~:text=Very%20few%20people%20are%20allowed,few%20do%20carry%20a%20weapon

21 https://en.wikipedia.org/wiki/Firearms_regulation_in_France

with a shooting club, completion of safety training, and passing psycho-logical evaluations.[22] The process is thorough to ensure that only re-sponsible individuals gain access to firearms.

Age Restrictions: The legal age for gun ownership is generally set at 18 years, with specific provisions for minors who are active in sport shoot-ing or hunting, allowing some exceptions under careful regulation.[23]

Restrictions on Carrying Firearms: Unlike some countries, France does not allow open carry of firearms in public places. Instead, firearms must be transported securely, usually unloaded, and stored in locked containers when in transit.

Health and Background Checks: Potential gun owners are subject to medical assessments, criminal background checks, and may also be list-ed on government blacklists if they have a history of violence or sub-stance abuse. This ensures that individuals who may pose a risk do not gain access to firearms.

Public Health and Safety Initiatives: There is an ongoing emphasis on public health campaigns aimed at promoting responsible gun ownership and awareness about the risks associated with firearms. These efforts are intended to mitigate accidents and encourage safe practices among gun owners.[24]

Enforcement: Violations of gun regulations, such as possession of illicit firearms or failure to comply with licensing requirements, can lead to significant penalties, including fines and imprisonment. Enforcement is undertaken by national police forces and local authorities who monitor compliance among gun owners.

---

22 https://www.thelocal.fr/20171004/
    five-things-to-know-about-guns-in-france

23 https://www.spectator.co.uk/article/
    what-the-french-get-right-about-guns/

24 https://www.statista.com/statistics/1246315/legal-firearms-france

Only few people are allowed to own firearms in France. Permitted groups include:

- Serving police officers, including those belonging to the police: *municipal, police de l'environnement, Vigipirate* and the *gendarmerie*;
- Judges, although very few do carry a weapon;
- Certain security guards, including some bodyguards;
- Hunters (permitted to obtain, transport, and use a gun, but only while hunting);
- People who are legally allowed to carry arms due to serious and precise threats to their personal safety and have decided not to employ the services of a bodyguard.

France's gun laws are designed to reduce the number of firearms in circulation and prevent illegal weapons from entering the country. To own a gun, individuals must first obtain a hunting or sporting license, which requires regular renewal, a psychological evaluation, and a clean criminal record. Civilians with the appropriate license are allowed to own up to seven .22 caliber handguns or five larger-caliber handguns, but a handgun purchase is only permitted after at least six months of membership in a shooting club affiliated with the French Shooting Federation. Firearms without a legitimate sporting or recreational use are strictly prohibited from entering the country.

Individuals purchasing firearms must declare the weapon to their local prefecture, where a risk assessment and background check will be conducted to ensure the buyer has no history of violent crimes or alcohol-related issues in the past 10 years. All private buyers, unlike those using firearms for professional purposes, must also register their weapon in the new system.

Traveling to France With a Firearm

Visitors seeking to bring firearms into France are met with stringent regulations that govern their entry and possession. According to French law, only certain categories of firearms may be imported, and even then, the process requires thorough documentation and permits. A valid reason for carrying a firearm must be established, which could range from participating in a sporting event to hunting, but personal protection is not regarded as an acceptable reason.

For visitors intending to bring firearms into France, securing an import permit is essential. This process begins with obtaining a Declaration of Intent from the French Customs Office, which must be accompanied by documents proving ownership and the purpose of bringing the firearm. Travelers must present any necessary sporting or hunting licenses from their home country that are recognized by French regulations travel information. Moreover, the firearm itself must comply with the European Firearms Pass regulation, if applicable.[25]

Visitors should also be aware that failing to comply with these legal requirements can lead to severe penalties, including confiscation of the firearm and potential criminal charges.

French authorities remain highly vigilant about the threat of terrorism and the potential role firearms may play in such acts. As a result, customs officers have the authority to inspect and verify all items upon entry, including checking permits related to firearms. The government routinely conducts security drills and engages in heightened surveillance, especially in areas frequented by tourists, to mitigate the risks associated with firearm possession.

25 https://travel.state.gov/content/travel/en/international-travel/
    International-Travel-Country-Information-Pages/France.html

Penalties

Violations of firearms laws in France can result in severe penalties, including fines and imprisonment. Authorities enforce these laws rigorously to maintain public safety and prevent firearms from falling into the wrong hands. Certain categories of individuals, such as minors and individuals with a history of mental illness or criminal activity, are prohibited from possessing firearms under French law.[26]

France maintains stringent firearms regulations to prioritize public safety, resulting in severe penalties for violations. The regulations classify firearms into categories A, B, C, and D, each with specific ownership requirements and associated penalties. For instance, possession of prohibited weapons in Category A can lead to up to 10 years in prison and fines of €500,000 (US$519,900) for trafficking offenses. In contrast, Category B firearms, which require authorization, can incur penalties of up to 5 years in prison and fines of €75,000 (US$77,985) if not properly licensed.

The illegal possession and trafficking of firearms are addressed rigorously, with illegal possession potentially leading to up to 3 years in prison and fines of €45,000 (US$46,791). Additionally, the importation of firearms is subject to strict guidelines, with violations resulting in confiscation and criminal charges. Carrying firearms without legal justification may incur fines up to €15,000 (US$15,597) and 1 year in prison.[27]

---

26 https://www.ojp.gov/pdffiles1/Digitization/131690NCJRS.pdf

27 https://www.gunpolicy.org/firearms/region/france

General Questions

1. *What happens if the police catch me carrying a firearm?*
Possession of firearms by those without permits is illegal and can carry heavy fines and prison sentences.

2. *Can foreigners bring firearms into France for personal use?*
Foreigners can bring firearms into France for personal use, but strict regulations apply. Travelers must declare their firearms at customs and provide the necessary documentation, such as a valid license from their home country and a reason for carrying the weapon (e.g., hunting or sport shooting). Additionally, the firearm must comply with French laws, and the traveler may need to obtain a temporary permit or authorization for the firearm to be legally brought into the country. It's essential to check the specific requirements before traveling, as failing to comply can lead to penalties or confiscation of the weapon.

Law of the Land Hypothetical

HYPOTHETICAL: *Johnathan traveled to France from the United States with a firearm in his checked luggage. He plans to have a fun and safe trip with his family and does not intend to use the firearm but brought it along for personal protection. Johnathan holds a concealed weapons permit from Florida. If the police stop him, will his Florida permit be recognized in France?*

ANSWER: **No.** *France has stringent regulations on firearms and ammunition. As a rule, firearms which have no legitimate sporting or recreational use are not permitted entry into France.*

Takeaways

- **Strict Regulations:** Firearm possession is highly regulated, requiring a valid hunting or sporting license, background checks, and psychological evaluations.

- **No Concealed Carry:** Foreign concealed carry permits are not valid in France. Firearms must be declared at customs with proper documentation.

- **Legal Process:** Travelers must follow legal procedures to bring firearms into France, including declaring them and proving their intended use.

- **Severe Penalties:** Illegal possession of firearms or ammunition can result in heavy fines, imprisonment, and weapon confiscation.

- **Ammunition Restrictions:** Ammunition is also strictly controlled, with limits on quantity and type for licensed individuals.

PROSTITUTION

IN THIS CHAPTER

PROSTITUTION

Overview[28]

In France, prostitution is legal, but the purchase of sexual services is criminalized. This shift began with the 1946 "loi de Marthe Richard" that closed brothels and adopted an abolitionist approach focused on protecting sex workers. Since April 2016, clients who engage with prostitutes can face fines or imprisonment. While sex work itself is legal, activities like pimping and running brothels are illegal, reflecting the government's effort to combat exploitation and promote public morality.

Laws and Penalties[29]

The French prostitution law enacted in 2016 is officially known as *"Loi no 2016-444 du 13 avril 2016 visant à renforcer la lutte contre le système prostitutionnel et à accompagner les personnes prostituées,"* which translates to "Law No. 2016-444 of April 13, 2016, aimed at strengthening the fight against the prostitution system and supporting prostituted persons." This law marked a significant shift in France's approach to

---

28 https://www.cnn.com/2016/04/07/europe/france-prostitution/index. html

29 https://www.thelocal.fr/20161027/ the-strangest-rules-from-frances-law-book

prostitution, emphasizing the criminalization of the purchase of sexual services while promoting support for those involved in sex work. The legislation aims to combat human trafficking and exploitation effectively while recognizing the rights and needs of sex workers seeking to exit the profession.

Key points of the French prostitution law:

- **Criminalized act:** Buying sexual acts is illegal.

- **Penalty for clients:** Fines up to €3,750 (US$3,899.25) for purchasing sex from an adult.

- **Aggravating factors:** Higher penalties apply if the sex worker is underage.

- **No criminalization of sex workers:** Selling sexual services is not illegal for sex workers.

- Paying for sex services carries a fine of €1,500 (US$1,559.70). Repeat offenders could be fined up to €3,750 (US$3,899.25).

 **Prostitution Practices**[30]

Sex work in France, like other countries takes many forms. These include street prostitution, escort services, bars, and apartment prostitution. Street prostitution is partly controlled by pimps, while other workers are autonomous prostitutes. In some areas, such as Lyon or the Bois de Boulogne in Paris, sex workers are also known to use vans.

The most famous street for prostitution in Paris, Rue Saint-Denis, has undergone some gentrification in recent years, pushing the sex workers further north. Compared to North America, escort services—where individuals hire someone for companionship or "entertainment," often including sex—are less prevalent in France. In bars, women attempt to persuade men into buying expensive drinks, often

---

30 https://en.wikipedia.org/wiki/Prostitution_in_France

in exchange for sexual favors. Prices are set by the bar owner, with the proceeds shared between the owner and the sex worker. Pigalle's peep-shows have gained notoriety for being involved in such scams.

Prostitution in apartments is often advertised in adult magazines and newspapers. Swingers' clubs, where partner-swapping takes place, may also host paid prostitutes alongside "amateur" women and couples. These establishments charge men a flat rate of around €80 to €120 (US$83.18 - $124.78), which covers food, drinks, and unlimited sexual encounters—many of which are performed in full view of all guests.

In France, the police approach to prostitution is largely centered on regulating and controlling activities associated with it, such as soliciting and procuring, rather than directly targeting the act of selling sex. This means that their primary focus is on intervening when prostitution is visibly occurring in public spaces or when there are concerns about trafficking or exploitation. They particularly focus on cracking down on individuals who facilitate prostitution, such as those managing brothels or acting as pimps.

Key Aspects of the Police Approach to Prostitution in France

Focus on Visibility:

Police primarily target street prostitution, as it is more visible and seen as disruptive to public order. Less visible forms of prostitution are often overlooked.

Anti-Trafficking Efforts:

A major part of police activity related to prostitution focuses on identifying and dismantling human trafficking networks that may be exploiting sex workers.

"Police des Mœurs":

France has historically had a specialized "vice squad" (*police des mœurs*) tasked with enforcing laws around prostitution. However, in recent years, the focus has shifted towards a more human rights-based approach.

 ## Sex Trafficking and Exploitation[31]

The fight against exploitation and human trafficking is one of France's priorities in terms of protecting and promoting human rights and fighting organized crime. For a decade, France has been implementing a dedicated public policy to fight human trafficking, to protect victims of all forms of exploitation with particular attention to the unconditional protection of children. Since 2016, France seen an increase of more than 48% in convictions for the human trafficking and exploitation offenses. In 2022, 1,046 people were convicted, illustrating a real improvement in awareness.

However, there is still much progress to be made. This is why the *National Plan to Combat Exploitation and Human Trafficking 2024-2027*, France's third plan of its kind, has been developed with the collaboration of the entire government. Presented alongside Olivier Dussopt, Minister of Labor, Full Employment, and Economic Inclusion, and Charlotte Caubel, Minister of State for Children, the plan aims to make significant strides in addressing the issue. In France, sexual exploitation remains the most prevalent form of human trafficking. The victims identified by internal security forces and supported by various organizations are predominantly women.

---

31 https://en.wikipedia.org/wiki/Human_trafficking_in_
France#:~:text=The%20Government%20of%20France%20
estimates,West%20Africa%2C%20and%20North%20Africa.

Vulnerable Areas

Certain areas of France are particularly vulnerable to sex trafficking due to a combination of factors such as economic disparities, high tourist activity, and the presence of marginalized communities. Urban centers like Paris, Nice, and Marseille experience increased trafficking due to their popularity with tourists, creating demand for commercial sex services. Economically disadvantaged regions, especially in northern France, see higher rates of poverty and unemployment, making individuals more susceptible to exploitation. Additionally, communities with significant immigrant populations are often targeted by traffickers who exploit their socio-economic challenges. Geographic proximity to international borders facilitates cross-border trafficking, while cities hosting major events and entertainment venues witness spikes in trafficking activities aligned with increased demand. Collectively, these factors underscore the complexities of combating sex trafficking in France, necessitating comprehensive prevention and support strategies tailored to the unique vulnerabilities of affected regions.

Sex Trafficking Demographics[32]

In France, the most vulnerable groups to human trafficking, due to their isolation, lack of resources and legal safeguards, are women, children, and unaccompanied minors. Women are the majority of victims, with an estimated 18,000 forced into prostitution, often manipulated or coerced by traffickers. Children, particularly from Romania, Africa, and the Middle East, are trafficked for sexual exploitation, frequently hidden in plain sight in France's sex trade. Unaccompanied minors, especially those from Comoros in Mayotte, are also at high risk. Lacking legal protection and support, they are easily targeted by traffickers, often forced into begging, criminal activity, or sexual exploitation.

---

32 https://tinyurl.com/msz5cy7t

Government Efforts[33]

The French government meets the minimum standards for eliminating human trafficking and maintains a Tier 1 ranking by the U.S. Department of State. It continues to identify more victims, implement a National Action Plan (NAP), and engage survivors to shape policy. A specialized cyber investigation unit is in place, and officials receive ongoing training.

While law enforcement participates in international investigations and arrests traffickers, fewer investigations and prosecutions occur for the fourth consecutive year.

Funding for victim assistance increases but remains insufficient, with NGOs helping fewer victims. The government does not provide compensation to victims and lacks a National Referral Mechanism (NRM) for consistent victim identification. Additionally, law enforcement continues to arrest child victims of forced begging and deport undocumented migrants from Mayotte without trafficking screenings.

Sex Tourism and Public Health Concerns[34]

Sex tourism is indeed present in France, particularly in major cities and regions that attract a significant influx of visitors seeking various forms of adult entertainment. Paris stands at the forefront as a prominent destination for sex tourism, with its well-known red-light districts, such as Pigalle, home to numerous sex shops, cabarets, and erotic venues like the iconic Moulin Rouge and Crazy Horse.[35] Additionally, cities like Nice and Marseille offer vibrant nightlife and an assortment of adult entertainment options, catering to tourists looking for a more libertine experience. Regions in the French Caribbean, such as Guadeloupe and Martinique, also see aspects of sex tourism as tourist demand intersects

---

33 https://www.state.gov/reports/2024-trafficking-in-persons-report/
france/

34 https://tinyurl.com/2j6rdv92

35 https://parisjetaime.com/eng/article/sexy-paris-a335

with local cultural expressions of sexuality. In these areas, sex tourism often intertwines with broader discussions about exploitation, safety, and human trafficking, making the phenomenon complex and multifaceted in nature.

Sex tourism is typically organized through a combination of specialized travel agencies and online platforms that cater to individuals seeking sexual services while traveling. These travel agencies offer adult-oriented packages that include accommodations, transportation, and guided tours to nightlife hotspots or brothels, utilizing targeted marketing strategies to attract clientele.[36] Additionally, online platforms and dating sites have become crucial in connecting individuals based on their interests, making it easier for tourists to find partners or services in their desired locations. Social media plays a vital role in advertising sex tourism, with operators promoting their offerings through enticing visuals and testimonials while influencers help to amplify their reach. Word of mouth remains an effective method of promotion, with travelers sharing experiences and recommendations within their social circles and online forums. Nevertheless, it's important to navigate the legal constraints and ethical considerations surrounding the sex tourism industry, as many countries have laws regulating prostitution and sex work. Responsible operators often emphasize the rights and safety of sex workers, promoting ethical practices to ensure a respectful and safe environment for all parties involved.

Sex tourism in France raises significant health concerns for both sex workers and clients. The primary risk involves the heightened spread of sexually transmitted infections (STIs), including HIV, due to inconsistent use of protection among patrons. This environment can lead to high-risk sexual behaviors, while access to healthcare often remains limited, further exacerbating the situation. Additionally, sex workers frequently experience mental health challenges related to stigma, violence, and exploitation, resulting in emotional trauma. Therefore, public health initiatives are essential to promote safe practices and provide support services that protect the well-being of all individuals involved in sex tourism.

---

36 https://www.dw.com/en/
france-ban-prostitution-sex-workers-threat/a-57198238

 **General Questions**

1. *Is selling sex criminalized?* Selling sex is legal in France, and national laws that previously criminalized soliciting were repealed when the country criminalized clients. However, municipal administrative laws—known as *"arrêtés"*—still exist, making it illegal for sex workers to operate in certain areas, such as on the streets. Additionally, laws against brothel-keeping and procuring mean sex workers cannot legally work together or allow a colleague to use their flat or camper for sex work.

2. *Is there mandatory HIV/STI testing or registration for sex workers in France?* No, there is neither mandatory HIV/STI testing nor registration for sex workers in France.

3. *Are there other laws that target sex workers in France?* Yes. In France, municipal by-laws are used to target sex workers. For example, one city has used these laws to effectively ban sex workers from the city center.

4. *Is there mandatory HIV/STI testing or registration for sex workers in France?* No, there is neither mandatory HIV/STI testing nor registration for sex workers in France.

5. *Is sex work recognized as work?* No, sex work is not officially recognized as work in France.

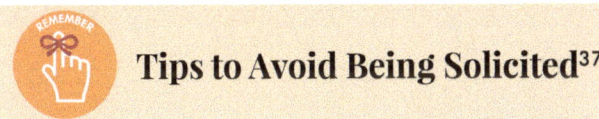

Tips to Avoid Being Solicited[37]

To avoid being solicited by sex workers in France, it's important to be assertive and take proactive steps to deter unwanted attention. Here's a summary of the key strategies:

- **Be Direct and Clear:** If approached, politely but firmly say "no thank you" and walk away.

- **Avoid Eye Contact:** In areas with high solicitation, avoiding direct eye contact can help prevent being approached.

- **Dress Modestly:** To avoid being perceived as an easy target, consider wearing conservative clothing, especially in areas known for solicitation.

- **Stick to Well-Lit, Populated Areas:** Stay in areas with more people and good lighting to reduce the chances of encountering solicitations in secluded spots.

- **Be Aware of Your Surroundings:** Stay alert to your environment and be prepared to move away if someone approaches.

Important Considerations:

- **Local Laws:** Prostitution laws can vary from city to city in France, so it's useful to be aware of the local regulations.

- **Respectful Interaction:** Always remain polite and respectful when declining an approach, as maintaining civility helps avoid unnecessary tension.

If you experience persistent harassment, contact local authorities for assistance.

---

37 https://tinyurl.com/yc7hbfht

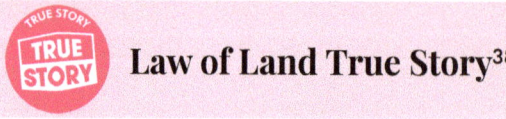

Law of Land True Story[38]

In 2022, after French authorities uncovered an apartment used for prostitution, an investigation revealed a network involved in human trafficking and sexual exploitation in both France and Spain. The victims, primarily from Latin America, the Caribbean, and Romania, were transported to France and then moved across the country to work in prostitution in short-term rental apartments controlled by the criminal group. The network also used the internet to advertise paid sexual services. Following the operation and the arrests of the suspects, six victims in France received support and shelter from a dedicated non-profit organization.

---

38 https://www.eurojust.europa.eu/news/
     eurojust-supports-arrest-nine-human-traffickers-france-and-spain

CHAPTER 8
LGBTQ

LGBTQ

Overview[39]

France is widely regarded as one of the most LGBTQ+-friendly countries in the world, with significant strides in legal reforms and societal acceptance over the past few decades. The country has progressively expanded rights for LGBTQ+ individuals, including legalizing same-sex marriage in 2013, decriminalizing transgender identity in 2010, and ensuring strong anti-discrimination protections.

Public opinion in France is generally supportive of LGBTQ+ rights, with a majority of the population backing same-sex marriage and social acceptance of homosexuality. Cities like Paris are celebrated for their vibrant LGBTQ+ communities and nightlife, especially in districts such as Le Marais. However, despite these advancements, challenges remain, including occasional incidents of discrimination and violence, which continue to prompt advocacy for greater equality and protection.

Homophobia in France

Despite being recognized for its progressive LGBTQ rights, France still grapples with rampant homophobia, as evidenced by a significant rise in reported incidents. Activist groups like *SOS Homophobie* have

---

39 https://www.cnn.com/2016/04/07/europe/france-prostitution/index.html

highlighted a troubling increase in hate crimes, with reports indicating nearly a 30% rise in homophobic attacks recently.[40]

This recent increase in homophobic hate crimes in France can be attributed to various factors, including the rise of far-right political movements that have emboldened discriminatory rhetoric and behavior against LGBTQ communities.[41] Additionally, heightened visibility of LGBTQ issues and activism may provoke backlash from certain segments of society, leading to increased hostility and violence.

Homophobia in France is expressed through various forms in daily life, impacting individuals across different social contexts. Verbal harassment remains prevalent, with LGBTQ individuals often facing derogatory slurs and insults in public spaces, workplaces, and educational settings. Discrimination also occurs in social environments like bars and restaurants, where same-sex couples may be subjected to hostile reactions or denial of service. Additionally, online platforms serve as venues for hate speech and cyberbullying, contributing to a toxic atmosphere for LGBTQ individuals. Institutional homophobia can manifest through discriminatory policies in education and healthcare, further exacerbating feelings of exclusion and marginalization within the community.

LGBTQ Legislation

France has established a comprehensive legal framework to protect LGBTQ rights, demonstrating its commitment to equality and inclusion. Key legislation includes the legalization of same-sex marriage in 2013, which allows same-sex couples to marry and adopt children with the same rights as heterosexual couples. Furthermore, anti-discrimination laws enacted in 1985 and 2012 explicitly prohibit discrimination based on sexual orientation and gender identity in various sectors, including employment and public services.

---

40 https://www.france24.com/en/europe/20230516-homophobic-attacks-in-france-rose-almost-30-percent-last-year-lgbtq-group-says

41 https://www.france24.com/en/live-news/20240516-french-lgbtq-groups-extremely-concerned-over-increase-in-attacks

In a progressive step for transgender rights, France amended its laws in 2017 to permit individuals to change their legal gender without the requirement of surgery or a medical diagnosis, although there is still ongoing discussion regarding the acknowledgment of non-binary identities. The country has also enacted hate crime legislation that imposes stricter penalties for crimes motivated by homophobia and transphobia, signaling a strong governmental stance against violence and discrimination.[42]

LGBTQ Tourism and Safety Concerns

LGBTQ tourism in France has experienced significant growth, driven by the country's progressive stance on LGBTQ rights and its vibrant local communities. **Paris** is the heart of this movement, with the *Marais* district serving as a central hub for LGBTQ life, featuring numerous bars, clubs, and events such as the annual *Paris Pride Parade*, which draws hundreds of thousands of attendees. **Nice** follows closely, known for its Mediterranean beaches and a lively LGBTQ-friendly atmosphere, particularly in the Old Town where venues like *Le Glam* thrive. **Lyon** is emerging as another key destination, boasting a growing LGBTQ scene and hosting events like the *Lyon Gay Pride*, while **Marseille** offers its own eclectic mix of bars and cultural experiences.

There are a few areas that may be unsafe for individuals in this community, particularly in conservative neighborhoods and smaller towns where homophobic attitudes persist. Reports indicate that urban regions, such as parts of eastern Paris, have seen incidents of violence against LGBTQ individuals, prompting many to avoid public displays of affection due to safety concerns. The rise of far-right rhetoric further exacerbates these risks, creating an atmosphere of fear among LGBTQ people in certain communities throughout the country.

LGBTQ visitors to France should remain aware of safety concerns due to the such anti-LGBTQ sentiment linked to far-right political movements, which can foster hostility in certain areas. It is advisable for travelers to research their destinations and exercise caution, particularly in rural

---

42 https://en.wikipedia.org/wiki/LGBTQ_rights_in_France

regions or conservative urban areas where acceptance may be somewhat limited.

General Questions

1. *Can same-sex couples legally adopt children in France?* **Yes.** Same-sex couples have been legally able to adopt children since May 2013, when the same-sex marriage law took effect. The first joint adoption by a same-sex couple was announced on October 18, 2013.

2. *Does France have discrimination laws protecting LGBTQ individuals?* **Yes.** Laws prohibiting discrimination based on sexual orientation were introduced in 1985, and gender identity protections were added in 2012. These laws cover areas such as employment, housing, healthcare, and public services, ensuring that LGBTQ+ people are protected from unfair treatment. Additionally, France has ratified several international agreements and conventions aimed at safeguarding the rights of LGBTQ+ individuals.

Law of the Land True Story[43]

On the corner of Rue Bachaumont and Rue Montorgueil in Paris, a plaque marks the location where Jean Diot and Bruno Lenoir were arrested on January 4th, 1750. A city watchman caught them having sex, and they were subsequently put on trial for homosexuality. They were executed on July 6th, 1750, and are remembered as the last people put to death in France for this crime. Forty-one years later, during

---

43 https://www.storyofacity.com/2020/06/30/
    celebrating-lgbtq-history-france/

the French Revolution, homosexuality was officially decriminalized in 1791, making France the first Western European country to do so. In 2010, France took another significant step by becoming the first country in the world to declassify transgenderism as a mental illness. While challenges remain in achieving full equality for LGBTQ+ citizens, these milestones represent historic advances in the recognition of LGBTQ+ rights in France.

Takeaways[44]

- Same-sex marriage legalized in 2013, granting adoption rights to same-sex couples.

- Anti-discrimination laws protecting sexual orientation (1985) and gender identity (2012).

- Transgender individuals can change legal gender without surgery or medical diagnosis (2017).

- France decriminalized homosexuality in 1791, becoming the first Western European country to do so.

- Paris and other cities like Nice and Lyon are known for their vibrant LGBTQ+ communities and events.

- Far-right political movements and heightened LGBTQ+ visibility contribute to backlash.

- Major LGBTQ+ tourist destinations include Paris, Nice, and Lyon.

- Areas like Le Marais in Paris and Old Town Nice are known for their LGBTQ+ nightlife and events.

- Rural and conservative areas may present safety concerns due to homophobic attitudes.

---

44 https://app.vaia.com/studyset/21193676/summary/71656859

SEXUALLY MOTIVATED/ VIOLENT CRIMES

SEXUALLY MOTIVATED/ VIOLENT CRIMES

Overview

Sexually-motivated crimes in France have seen a significant increase, with approximately 94,900 offenses reported in 2023, up from around 84,500 in 2022, reflecting a troubling upward trend since 2016.[45] The majority of victims are women, making up 85% of reported cases, while 96% of perpetrators are men.[46] Despite the increasing visibility of these crimes, a substantial number remain unreported, with only about 6% of victims of physical sexual violence filing complaints. Influenced by social movements like #MeToo, more individuals are coming forward, but underreporting continues to obscure the true prevalence of sexual violence in France.

Sexually-motivated crimes in France exhibit significant regional disparities influenced by various socio-economic, cultural, and demographic factors. Urban areas, particularly cities like Paris and Marseille, report higher instances of sexual offenses, attributed to larger populations, anonymity, and socio-economic challenges such as increased

45 https://www.statista.com/statistics/1418831/sexual-offences-france

46 https://www.lemonde.fr/en/les-decodeurs/article/2024/11/25/rape-assault-harassment-what-do-the-numbers-show-about-violence-against-women-in-france_6734019_8.html

unemployment that correlate with higher rates of sexual violence. Conversely, rural regions typically show lower reported rates, reflecting potential underreporting due to social stigma and cultural norms discouraging discussions about such crimes. The rise of the #MeToo movement has facilitated greater reporting, particularly in regions with robust community awareness, while areas with conservative attitudes may perpetuate cycles of silence around victimization.

Related Legislation

In France, the legal framework surrounding sexually motivated crimes is primarily governed by the Penal Code. Sexual offenses, including sexual harassment, sexual assault, and rape, have been criminalized under various articles of the code. Specifically, Article 222-33 defines sexual harassment, while Articles 222-22 to 222-27 delineate the specifics of sexual assault and rape.[47]

The introduction of the "Loi n° 2018-703" in 2018 marked a substantial shift in France's approach to sexual violence. This law aimed to enhance protections for victims and includes provisions that redefine consent, making it clear that any sexual act with a person under 18 years of age is considered a crime, irrespective of alleged consent.

The penalties associated with sexually-motivated crimes in France vary significantly based on the severity of the offense, with sexual harassment punishable by up to two years in prison and €30,000 (US$31,194) in fines, while serious offenses like rape can result in up to twenty years of imprisonment or life sentences for aggravated cases. Importantly, French law also allows for civil damages claims during the penal trial, which is distinct from many other legal systems where civil cases are separate.

Enforcement is carried out by a combination of police, judiciary, and support organizations, emphasizing the importance of prompt reporting by victims. Specialized police units trained in handling sexual violence cases play a crucial role in supporting victims, ensuring their complaints

---

47 https://shs.cairn.info/article/E_TGS_028_0089?lang=en

are taken seriously. Additionally, the courts have been urged to impose more severe penalties for repeat offenders to serve as a deterrent.

 **Reporting an Incident to Police**

If you are the victim of a sexual crime in France, there are several steps you can take. First, if you have a tour guide, they can arrange for support. If you're near your embassy or consulate, consular staff can accompany you to the police station or provide other assistance. You can report the crime by calling the police at **112** (mobile) or **17** (landline), where an interpreter will be provided if necessary. Alternatively, you can visit a police station (*commissariat de police or brigade de gendarmerie*), email the OCRVP at **ocrvp@interieur.gouv.fr**, or report through the Ma Sécurité portal for sexual or gender-based violence.

It's important to report the crime as soon as possible to preserve forensic evidence. Avoid washing or changing clothes before a forensic examination. If you change clothes, be sure to bring the ones you were wearing when the crime occurred. When filing a complaint, police will record the details, and they may assist you in obtaining a medical examination. If there has been physical assault, the police may take you to a medical-legal emergency unit for further examination. A doctor will check for injuries, DNA traces, and signs of drug use (e.g., GHB), and may conduct tests for HIV, pregnancy, or other concerns. A medical certificate will be provided.

Regarding the police investigation, the Public Prosecutor (*Procureur de la République*) will determine the next steps. If there is overwhelming evidence, such as a confession, a fast-track trial may be ordered. If there is insufficient evidence, the case may be dismissed, but this doesn't mean that nothing happened. Alternatively, further investigation may be required, and an Examining Magistrate (*Juge d'Instruction*) will continue the inquiry.

General Questions

1. *Do laws in France related to sex crimes protect males and females equally?* **Yes**, they provide protection to both genders equally.

2. *What is the age of consent for sex in France?* The age of consent in France is **15 years old.** The age of consent is the minimum age at which an individual is considered legally old enough to consent to participation in sexual activity. Individuals aged 14 or younger in France are not legally able to consent to sexual activity, and such activity may result in prosecution for statutory rape or the equivalent local law.[48]

Law of the Land Hypothetical

HYPOTHETICAL: *Sophie, a 25-year-old student, was traveling alone on a train from Paris to Lyon. During the journey, she was sexually harassed by a man sitting next to her. Despite her attempts to move away and ignore the behavior, the man persisted, making inappropriate comments and gestures. What should Sophie do?*

ANSWER: *Sophie should first prioritize her safety by moving to a different seat or carriage if she feels threatened. She should then immediately notify train staff, as most trains in France have personnel available to assist with such situations. If the harassment continues or she feels it's necessary, Sophie can report the incident to the police upon arrival at her destination. French law enforcement takes harassment and assault on public transport seriously and can help her understand her legal options, such as filing a police report, seeking a restraining order, or pursuing criminal charges.*

---

48 https://www.ageofconsent.net/world/france
https://www.womenlobby.org/IMG/pdf/2714_france_lr.pdf

CHAPTER 10
ARRESTED IN FRANCE

CHAPTER 10
ARRESTED IN FRANCE

Overview

When traveling in a foreign country, it's imperative to recognize you are subject to the legal jurisdiction and regulations of that nation. These laws may significantly differ from those in your home country and might not offer the same legal protections you are accustomed to. It's crucial to bear in mind that penalties for violating foreign laws can be more severe than those for similar offenses in your home country, and ignorance of these laws is not typically accepted as a defense.

The consequences of breaking the law while abroad can be severe and may include expulsion, fines, arrest, or imprisonment. Even unintentional violations can lead to serious legal repercussions. It is essential for travelers to be aware of and adhere to the laws of the host country to avoid legal entanglements and ensure a safe and enjoyable experience.

Specifically, stringent penalties are often enforced for possession, use, or trafficking of illegal drugs in many countries. Convicted offenders can expect severe consequences, including lengthy jail sentences and hefty fines. The legal processes for foreigners in the event of an arrest abroad involve being charged or indicted, prosecuted, potentially convicted and sentenced, and, if applicable, going through an appeals process.

Navigating a foreign legal system can be complex, and individuals arrested abroad must be prepared to comply with the legal procedures of the host country. Seeking legal representation and understanding the local legal nuances are crucial steps for those facing legal issues in a foreign jurisdiction.

Awareness of and adherence to the laws of a foreign country are paramount when traveling. Understanding the potential consequences for legal violations and being prepared to navigate the legal system of the host country are essential aspects of responsible international travel.

 ## Arrest Process[49]

French criminal law categorizes offenses into three main classes: contraventions (minor offenses), *délits* (mid-level offenses), and *crimes* (serious offenses). Contraventions include lesser violations, such as traffic offenses and public disturbances, typically resulting in fines. Délits encompass more serious crimes like theft, fraud, and assault, with penalties ranging from up to three years for simple theft to five years for significant fraud. Crimes, the most severe category, include offenses like murder and sexual violence, which can incur penalties of life imprisonment, particularly for premeditated actions or aggravated circumstances. The penalties for these offenses reflect France's commitment to public safety and justice, addressing both minor and serious crimes through a structured legal approach. Understanding the nature and consequences of these offenses is crucial for navigating the French legal system and ensuring societal order.

Following an arrest in France, the individual enters a structured legal process governed by the French criminal justice system. Initially, the arrested person is placed in police custody (*garde à vue*), which typically lasts for 24 hours but can be extended for another 24 hours with the authorization of a public prosecutor in more serious cases. During this period, the individual must be informed of their rights, which include the right to legal representation, the right to remain

---

49 https://www.sba-avocats.com/criminal-defense-attorney-paris-france-police-custody.html

silent, and the right to inform a family member or loved one. Police interrogations are conducted to gather evidence and information related to the alleged crime. Following the custody period, the detainee is presented before a judge, who then examines the circumstances of the case, determines whether to release the individual, impose bail, or order pre-trial detention based on the evidence and charges.[50] This structured process reflects the French commitment to due process and the protection of individual rights within the judicial system.

Rights of the Arrested Person[51]

When placed under police custody in France, a detainee must be immediately informed of their rights in a language they understand, with a translator provided if necessary. These rights include:

1. **Right to Information:** The detainee must be informed of the purpose of their detention, its expected duration, and the specific criminal offense they are suspected of committing, including details about when and where it occurred.

2. **Right to Legal Assistance:** The detainee has the right to be assisted by a lawyer from the moment they are detained.

3. **Right to Medical Examination:** The detainee can request to be examined by a physician to ensure their health permits them to remain in custody.

4. **Right to Notify Family or Employer:** A detainee can have a relative, employer, or embassy informed of their detention, unless the prosecutor delays this to avoid compromising evidence.

---

50 https://www.prison-insider.com/en/france/
en-cas-d-arrestation-5798a4664e206

51 https://www.sba-avocats.com/criminal-defense-attorney-paris-france-po-
lice-custody.html

5. **Right to Access Case Documents:** The detainee may consult certain documents related to the investigation, such as police interrogation transcripts and medical certificates.

6. **Right to Forward Comments:** The detainee can submit comments to the prosecutor or judge before any decision is made about extending their detention.

7. **Right to Remain Silent:** During interrogations, the detainee has the right to answer questions or remain silent after declaring their identity.

Detainees have the right to a lawyer at any time during police custody. The lawyer can assist during interrogations and confrontations. However, if the public prosecutor deems it necessary for the investigation, they can delay the detainee's access to a lawyer for up to 12 hours. In cases involving offenses punishable by five years or more in prison, the prosecutor can extend this delay to 24 hours, but only with authorization from a judge. If this right is violated (e.g., for an offense punishable by less than five years), any statements made without a lawyer present may not be admissible in court.

Getting Legal Assistance

If you are a foreign national, you should notify your embassy or consulate immediately. American citizens can do so using the *American Citizens Services Contact Form* found at **https://fr.usembassy.gov/contact/**. The embassy can help contact family, friends, or employers of the detained U.S. citizen with their written consent, visit the detained U.S. citizen in jail, help ensure that prison officials provide appropriate medical care, explain the local criminal justice and legal processes, and most importantly, connect you to local attorneys who speak English (a list of English-speaking attorneys can be accessed at **https://fr.usembassy. gov/local-resources/**). Bear in mind, however, that their powers are limited, and they cannot get U.S. citizens out of jail, provide legal advice, or represent U.S. citizens in court, serve as official interpreters or translators, nor can they pay your legal, medical, or other fees.[52]

U.S. Embassy in Paris

2 Avenue Gabriel

75008 Paris, France

Phone: +(33)(1) 43-12-22-22

Website: https://fr.usembassy.gov/contact/

The growing demand for legal services among the English-speaking community has led to an increase in the availability of English-speaking lawyers, particularly in major cities like Paris, Nice, and Lyon. Besides the home embassy or consulate, resources to locate these lawyers include the *Paris Bar Association*'s online directory, which allows searches based on language and expertise, as well as dedicated platforms like *Angloinfo* and *AIEL*, which list reputable law firms catering to English speakers.

Paris Bar Association

11 Place Dauphine

75001 Paris, France

Phone: +33 (0)1 44 32 48 00

Email: contact@barreaudeparis.org

Website: https://eutrp.eu/entities/entities-92/

Bail[53]

The bail system in France operates under a framework that emphasizes judicial oversight and the right to presumption of innocence. In the French legal system, instead of traditional bail as seen in common law jurisdictions, pre-trial measures such as placement under judicial supervision or *"contrôle judiciaire"* are utilized. This allows for individuals to

---

52   https://fr.usembassy.gov/services/arrest-of-a-u-s-citizen/

53   https://www.fairtrials.org/wp-content/uploads/France-advice-note.pdf

remain free under certain conditions set by a judge, including limitations on travel or requirements to report regularly to authorities.[54]

When a person is arrested, they may be held in custody if deemed necessary for the investigation, but the usage of pre-trial custody should be exceptional—a principle enshrined in the law—as France's justice system aims to balance the need for public safety with protecting individual rights. If a judge finds that release is appropriate, they may impose conditions rather than monetary bail to ensure court appearance and compliance with judicial oversight. The absence of bail bondsmen means defendants cannot secure release through financial means, instead relying on judicial assessments. This system aims to protect public safety and maintain the integrity of the legal process, reducing the risk of individuals evading legal responsibility. Additionally, it avoids potential abuses linked to financial disparities, promoting fairness and equality in the legal system.

 ## Complaints Against Police

The reputation of the French police force is characterized by a blend of trust and criticism, with about 70 percent of the public expressing confidence in law enforcement, particularly among older individuals.[55] However, significant concerns persist regarding systemic discrimination and allegations of police brutality, particularly against marginalized communities, which contribute to mistrust. This duality of perception is reflected in the societal discourse surrounding police practices, as many citizens advocate for reforms to improve accountability and foster better community relations.

The most common complaints against the French police force revolve around systemic discrimination, particularly against Black and Arab

---

54 https://www.growthinktank.org/en/
    pre-trial-custody-in-france-preventive-or-excessive

55 https://www.statista.com/statistics/1004491/
    trust-level-national-police-france

individuals, and allegations of police brutality during arrests and protests. Many people report experiencing ethnic profiling through discriminatory stop-and-search practices, which exacerbate feelings of mistrust within minority communities. Additionally, a significant concern is the lack of accountability and transparency regarding police misconduct, making it difficult for victims to seek justice. These issues not only undermine public trust in law enforcement but also hinder effective community relations and overall public safety in France.[56]

To file a complaint against the police in France, individuals can choose from several options. Complaints can be submitted in person at a police station or *gendarmerie,* where you must present necessary documents and formally sign your complaint.[57]

Alternatively, for certain cases involving property violations or where the perpetrator is unknown, you can file an online pre-complaint through the Pre-plainte-en-ligne. gouv.fr service.[58]

Additionally, you have the option to submit a complaint by post to the public prosecutor at the judicial court where the incident occurred. It is essential to provide detailed information about the incident, including dates, circumstances, and any evidence available to support your claim.

---

56 https://apnews.com/article/
    france-racism-police-id-checks-d3e3afa3c9e8981605b882c13e4110a2

57 https://www.service-public.fr/particuliers/vosdroits/F1435?lang=en

58 https://www.masecurite.interieur.gouv.fr/en/procedures/online-complain

General Questions

1. *Can I contact my embassy or consulate?* **Yes**, as a foreign national, you have the right to contact your embassy or consulate. They can provide consular assistance, including information on local legal processes and help with communication.

2. *How long can I be held in custody?* You can be held in police custody (*garde à vue*) for **up to 24 hours.** This can be extended for another 24 hours (48 hours total) with authorization from a prosecutor. For serious offenses, it may be extended further, up to 6 days, with approval from a judge.

3. *Will I have to appear in court?* If you are formally charged with a crime in France, you will typically have to appear in court for your trial. The court will determine the outcome of the case based on the evidence presented. However, if you are released on bail, you may attend the trial as required. In some cases, if you are not in custody, you may still be required to appear in court to answer charges.

4. *What happens if I don't speak French?* You have the right to request a translator if you do not speak French. Authorities are required to provide translation services to ensure you understand the proceedings.

5. *Can I leave France if I'm under investigation or awaiting trial?* It depends on the specifics of your case and any travel restrictions imposed by the court. It's advisable to consult with legal counsel and your embassy regarding your ability to leave the country.

 # Law of the Land Hypothetical

HYPOTHETICAL: *John, a 30-year-old tourist visiting Paris, was celebrating with friends at a local bar. He had a bit too much to drink and was found by police officers behaving disorderly on a public street near the bar. What should John do?*

ANSWER: *If John is arrested for public intoxication in France, he should remain calm and fully cooperate with the police. It's important to follow their instructions to avoid escalating the situation. John should ask the officers to clarify the charges and explain the legal consequences. Public intoxication (ivresse publique) can result in a fine or temporary detention to sober up. John should provide his ID and any necessary information when requested. Cooperation and honesty can help resolve the situation smoothly. Depending on the local procedures, he may be given the option to pay a fine immediately or might need to await further processing, which could include a court appearance or other administrative steps.*

 # Law of the Land True Story

Pavel Durov, the founder and CEO of the messaging app Telegram, was arrested in France in August 2024. Durov was arrested at Paris-Le Bourget Airport after arriving from Azerbaijan. Durov was charged with a range of crimes related to alleged illicit activity on Telegram, including drug trafficking and child sexual abuse. Durov was released after four days of questioning and ordered to pay five million euros in bail. He was also directed to report to a police station twice a week. Telegram said that it abides by EU laws and that Durov has nothing to hide.

JAILS VS. PRISONS: CONDITIONS & CULTURE

CHAPTER 11

JAILS VS. PRISONS: CONDITIONS & CULTURE

Overview

France's penal system consists of around 190 institutions, including remand prisons for those awaiting trial and correctional facilities for convicted offenders. As of 2024, the prison population has reached alarming levels, often exceeding 125% of capacity, which results in overcrowding and inadequate resources for rehabilitation.[59] Governed by the Ministry of Justice, the system aims to promote reintegration and reduce recidivism; however, it faces significant challenges related to treatment conditions and allegations of discrimination against specific groups.

The primary purpose of jails and prisons in France is to ensure public safety through the confinement of individuals who have committed crimes while facilitating their reintegration into society. Additionally, French penal institutions serve distinct functions: jails primarily hold individuals awaiting trial, while prisons accommodate those serving sentences, with a focus on maintaining order and security while respecting the rights of inmates. Additional key differences include security levels, with jails generally having fewer restrictions compared to prisons, and the range of programs offered, as prisons provide more comprehensive rehabilitation services due to longer incarceration periods.

---

59   https://www.prisonstudies.org/country/france#:~:text=Occupancy%20
level%20%28based%20on%20official%20capacity%29%20125.8%25

France's jails and prisons face several critical challenges. One of the most pressing issues is rampant overcrowding, with facilities often operating at or above 125% capacity, which exacerbates tensions among inmates and strains resources.[60] Additionally, there are concerns regarding inadequate mental health care and rehabilitation programs, limiting opportunities for inmates to reintegrate into society successfully. Incidents of violence, both between inmates and against staff, are also prevalent, further complicating the management of these facilities. Lastly, systemic discrimination, particularly against marginalized communities, undermines the integrity of the penal system and raises significant concerns regarding equity and justice in incarceration practices.

Prison Conditions and Living Environment

The French prison system is structured into various housing units based on the nature of inmates' offenses, security risk, and rehabilitation needs. These units aim to ensure safety while promoting reintegration into society.

- **Remand Prisons** (*Maisons d'Arrêt*): For individuals awaiting trial or serving short sentences (less than two years). These prisons have fewer resources and a high turnover of inmates.

- **Detention Centers** (*Centres de Détention*): For inmates serving medium-length sentences who have committed less severe offenses. They offer more rehabilitation programs.

- **Security Prisons** (*Maisons Centrales*): For long-term inmates (over 10 years) with higher security risks due to the severity of their crimes. These facilities have stricter controls and fewer privileges.

- **Day-Leave Centers** (*Centres de Semi-Liberté*): For inmates nearing the end of their sentences who can leave the prison during the day for work or rehabilitation but return at night.

---

60 https://www.rfi.fr/en/france/20241203-french-prison-crisis-deepens-with-cells-holding-four-times-capacity

- **Open Units:** Less common, these units allow inmates to live in shared apartments, focusing on rehabilitation and gradual reintegration into society.

Under French law, prisoners have the right to access health care services equivalent to those available in the community. Each prison is equipped with a medical infirmary that provides basic medical services, including periodic physical examinations, vaccinations, and essential treatments. Moreover, inmates in need of specialized medical care can be referred to external facilities, ensuring they receive treatment for conditions beyond the scope of prison health services.

However, despite these legal provisions, reports indicate that access to health care is often limited by various factors, including staffing shortages, inadequate facilities, and systemic inefficiencies that hinder timely and effective medical interventions. For example, the ratio of medical professionals to inmates is notably low, often resulting in infrequent consultations and generalized care that fails to address specific health needs.

Mental health care and substance abuse treatment in French prisons face significant challenges, stemming from overcrowded conditions and a shortage of qualified professionals. Many inmates grapple with psychological disorders and addiction issues, yet access to adequate treatment remains limited, often resulting in a cycle of neglect and deterioration of their health.

French law mandates that prisons provide meals that meet strict hygiene and nutritional standards, considering inmates' health and dietary needs. However, budget constraints and mismanagement often result in inadequate food quality, with reports of unsanitary meals and unbalanced nutrition, which can worsen inmates' health problems.

In addition to food, prisons are required to provide clean clothing, personal hygiene products, and medical care. However, overcrowding and underfunding have led to shortages in basic necessities, compromising inmate dignity and health. Issues such as inadequate bedding, poor sanitation, and overcrowded cells exacerbate hygiene-related problems and increase the risk of health issues. Furthermore, the system faces frequent criticism from human rights organizations and the European Court of Human Rights for failing to uphold basic rights, highlighting the urgent need for reforms that prioritize humane treatment and effective rehabilitation.

Inmate Rights and Legal Protections

Inmates in France are entitled to several important rights under French law, which are designed to ensure their dignity and well-being while incarcerated. These rights include the right to humane treatment and respect for their dignity, protection from inhumane and degrading treatment as stipulated by the French Constitution and international human rights agreements. Inmates have the right to access adequate health care, ensuring they receive medical treatment equivalent to that available in the community, which includes both physical and mental health services. Additionally, prisoners are entitled to legal aid and representation, enabling them to effectively navigate the judicial system and defend their rights. They also have the right to maintain contact with their families and friends, allowing for social connections that are crucial for emotional support and rehabilitation.[61] Furthermore, inmates can participate in various cultural, educational, and recreational activities designed to aid their rehabilitation and prepare them for reintegration into society.

Inmates in France have the right to access legal resources and court appeals, which is a fundamental component of ensuring justice and the protection of their legal rights. Under French law, specifically Article 1 of the Code of Criminal Procedure, prisoners are entitled to legal assistance, allowing them to seek representation and guidance during legal proceedings. This access to legal resources is crucial for inmates to understand their rights, navigate the complexities of the judicial system, and mount effective defenses against charges or prison conditions. Additionally, prisoners have the right to appeal court decisions, providing them with the opportunity to challenge verdicts or sentences they

---

61 https://www.prisonobservatory.org/index.
php?option=com_content&view=article&id=15&Itemid=119

believe to be unjust. However, the effectiveness of these rights can be hindered by factors such as limited access to legal aid services, which can result in disparities in representation and support for inmates seeking to exercise their legal rights.

Numerous reports of abuse in French prisons, including violence, overcrowding, and inadequate conditions, highlight the inhumane treatment of inmates. Human rights organizations like Amnesty International and Human Rights Watch have documented such abuse, including mistreatment by staff. Inmates have the right to seek legal aid for pursuing claims of abuse, although the effectiveness of these recourse options can vary. Inmates can report abuse through internal mechanisms, such as verbal communication with staff or written complaints to prison authorities, who are required to document them. Inmates are encouraged to provide detailed records of incidents, including dates, times, and witnesses. However, concerns about bias and obstacles within the system may hinder effective reporting. If internal procedures fail or inmates feel unsafe, they can seek external support from human rights organizations like the Defender of Rights, which help guide the reporting process. They can also submit complaints to judicial authorities or oversight bodies, such as the European Court of Human Rights, for further investigation and accountability.

 ## General Questions

1. *What is the difference between a jail and prison in France?* In France, jails (*maisons d'arrêt*) are short-term detention facilities for individuals awaiting trial or serving sentences of less than two years. Prisons (*maisons centrales, centres de détention*) are long-term facilities for inmates serving longer sentences, typically over two years, and are designed for more serious offenders.

2. *Do jails and prisons offer religious services to inmates?* In theory, French prisons are required to provide access to various religious practices, including Christian, Muslim, Jewish, and other faiths, in accordance with the principle of freedom of religion. Religious services are typically organized by chaplains and are available to inmates who wish to participate. However, while some prisons offer such programs, others do not, depending on the administration's perspective on their value, as well as the availability of sufficient staff and volunteers to run them. Additionally, space constraints can sometimes limit the provision of religious services.

3. *How do prisoners spend their time?* A typical day for a prisoner normally depends on their classification level. A prisoner whose crimes and behavior qualify them for low or medium security classification typically have more freedom and opportunities than those with high security classifications.

4. *How does the prison commissary system work in France?* The commissary system allows inmates to purchase basic goods like toiletries, snacks, and personal items using funds in their personal accounts. These accounts are typically funded by money sent from family members, earnings from prison work, or other external sources. The selection of items available in the commissary is limited and varies by prison, with luxury items being prohibited. Inmates can order items through a catalog, and deliveries are made on a regular basis. Prices tend to be higher than outside prison due to logistical costs, and financial constraints can limit access for inmates without outside support. Access to the commissary may also be restricted as a disciplinary measure, and the types of items available can depend on the security level of the facility.

Law of the Land True Story

John Miller, a U.S. Citizen, was arrested, tried, and convicted of petit theft in France. After Mr. Miller completes his sentence, he will be deported to the U.S. In minor cases, where it's not worth the time and trouble to go through a trial or house the person in prison, a country will simply deport the person, and bar him/her from returning. In either case, the U.S. Embassy may help to ensure that the person is treated no worse than a citizen of the foreign country would be while detained, help him/her find a local attorney, communicate with the person's family, etc.

HELPING A FRIEND OR RELATIVE IMPRISONED IN FRANCE

HELPING A FRIEND OR RELATIVE IMPRISONED IN FRANCE

Overview

If a family member or friend finds themselves imprisoned while visiting France, it can be a distressing situation for everyone involved. Understanding the legal framework and available support services is crucial to navigating this challenging ordeal. The first step in dealing with an arrest abroad is to gather detailed information about the arrest, including the reasons, charges, and location of detention. Contacting local authorities and the home embassy is crucial to obtain accurate information. Consular officials can offer guidance on legal rights, connect families with legal resources, and facilitate communication with the detained individual.

Securing competent legal representation is vital. Family members or friends should help find a qualified lawyer, typically through the local bar association or legal aid organizations. A lawyer ensures the individual's rights are protected and prepares a strong defense.

Maintaining communication with the imprisoned person is essential for emotional support. Families can send letters, emails, or care packages according to prison regulations, and in some cases, make authorized phone calls. Additionally, specialized organizations can offer emotional support, resources, and legal guidance to families. These groups may also advocate for better treatment and prison conditions when necessary.

For information related to the role of the U.S. Embassy in Paris and the list of English-speaking attorneys in France, please refer to *Chapter 10: Arrested in France.*

Getting Food to an Inmate

In France, prisoners are entitled to sufficient and nutritious meals that meet human rights standards, ensuring their health is maintained. Meals must be wholesome, balanced, and served with clean drinking water. However, budget limitations often impact the quality and quantity of food provided, with authorities typically allocating less than four euros per prisoner per day, leading to smaller portions and lower-quality meals.

French prisons strive to accommodate cultural and dietary needs, such as offering halal meals for Muslim prisoners, though implementation is inconsistent. A court ruling mandated halal meals at one facility, but not all prisons comply equally, raising concerns about equality in dietary provisions.

Despite regulations, prison food often falls short in quality, with many inmates describing it as monotonous and unappetizing. Meals are frequently criticized for being bland and poorly prepared. Some prisoners attempt to improve their meals by purchasing ingredients from the prison canteen, though some items are restricted for security reasons.[62]

While it is possible to send food to an inmate in a French prison, there are strict regulations govern this process. In general, food packages can be sent only if they conform to specific penitentiary conditions and must comply with hygiene and safety standards. To send food, individuals must first contact the specific prison to understand their rules and any restrictions regarding the types of food allowed. Typically, this involves completing a designated package form and including the inmate's identification number and the prison's address on the package label. It's

---

62 https://www.vice.com/en/article/
    prison-food-inmates-cooking-dany-hellz-kitchen

also important to ensure that the food items are properly packaged to prevent spoilage and adhere to any weight limits outlined by the prison. Note that food packages may only be allowed during certain times, such as holidays or special occasions, so checking with the prison administration is crucial for compliance.[63]

While the regulations indicate that visitors can bring food, there are restrictions on the types of food that can be delivered to inmates. For instance, home-cooked meals are usually prohibited as they could pose health risks and complicate security protocols. Instead, prisoners may receive commercially prepared foods that meet health and safety standards, thus ensuring the meals do not introduce unsanitary conditions into the prison environment. Prisons often distribute a list of acceptable food items to visitors, which includes non-perishable goods, snacks, and certain beverages.

The process for bringing food into French prisons typically involves submissive scrutiny. Before the delivery takes place, the food must be inspected by prison staff, who check for compliance with established regulations. Visitors may be required to fill out forms detailing the items they wish to bring and submit them for review prior to a scheduled visit. Additionally, most prisons have designated times and specific areas where food deliveries can be made.[64]

 ## Sending Money and Packages

Money

Due to the basic nature of the provisions provided by prisons, it is common for prisoners to request spending money to purchase additional groceries and toiletries. Although you can transfer money through

---

63 https://www.prison-insider.com/en/france/
    en-cas-d-arrestation-5798a4664e206

64 https://www.prisonobservatory.org/index.
    php?option=com_content&view=article&id=15&Itemid=119

family or friends in France, The U.S. Embassy can also help by setting up an Overseas Citizen's Trust, or OCS. The OCS is a special account designed to help individuals in the U.S. send money to friends or family members abroad who are incarcerated or in need. Setting up an OCS trust for a specific individual requires an initial US$30 fee. There are three ways to contribute to the OCS Trust: by overnight or regular mail, through a bank wire transfer, or using Western Union, which is typically the fastest method.

 If you have additional questions regarding the OCS Trust, call 202-647-5225, Monday through Friday, from 8 a.m. to 10 p.m., and Saturday from 9 a.m. to 3 p.m.

The process of sending money to inmates in French prisons is governed by specific regulations that prioritize security and transparency. As of January 1, 2019, wire transfers have become the primary means by which inmates can receive money from external sources. Family members or friends looking to send money must first contact the prison's registrar to obtain the specific bank account details necessary for such transfers. It is important to indicate the inmate's name and prison number in the transfer order to ensure proper crediting to the inmate's account.

In some instances, prisoners may also receive money via checks addressed to the prison accountant, although this method is less common and not universally accepted. Therefore, before initiating a transfer or sending a check, it is prudent to confirm with the prison administration whether these methods are permissible. Additionally, individuals who do not have a conventional bank account may utilize rechargeable payment cards that allow transfers to prisoners.

The French penal system has established strict regulations surrounding money transfers to inmates to prevent abuse and ensure financial integrity within prison. For instance, each inmate is allowed a maximum of €183 (US$190.28) per month once convicted, although defendants can receive unlimited funds during their pre-trial detention.

Moreover, it is important to note that cash payments or direct cash deposits are explicitly prohibited in French prisons. This restriction aims to control the flow of money and reduce the risks associated with trafficking and money laundering. Consequently, all transactions must be documented and processed through authorized banking channels to maintain accountability and security.

Packages

Sending packages to inmates is subject to strict regulations designed to maintain security and order within the correctional facilities. Visitors are generally allowed to send care packages, but these items must adhere to specific guidelines set forth by the prison administration. Typically, the package must be pre-approved, and it often needs to be sent via authorized third-party service providers to ensure compliance with established security protocols. Additionally, some prisons impose restrictions on the types of items that can be included, limiting them to permissible goods such as hygiene products or clothing, while prohibiting items deemed dangerous, such as sharp objects or any contraband.[65] Furthermore, there are often weight and size limitations, with many facilities setting a maximum weight of approximately 5 kilograms for packages.[66] Consequently, individuals wishing to send packages should familiarize themselves with the specific rules of the respective prison, as regulations can vary widely depending on the facility and the security classification of the inmate.

Visiting and Phone Calls

Visitation

To visit an inmate, you must request and obtain a visitation permit. This request can be submitted in writing or completed online, and supporting

---

65 https://www.eurosender.com/en/cp/care-package/prison

66 https://www.gov.uk/government/publications/france-prisoner-pack/ information-pack-for-british-nationals-arrested-or-detained-in-france

documents, such as identification photos, civil status documents, and proof of family ties, are required.

- Visitation permits for court proceedings are granted by the examining magistrate.
- Visitation permits for inmates are granted by the prison administration.

Each penitentiary establishment has its own contact information, which can be found in the Ministry of Justice's directory. Some facilities also provide phone numbers for arranging prison visits.

Phone Calls

Inmates are not permitted to receive phone calls from outside the prison. However, in certain situations, loved ones may contact the penitentiary integration and probation services to relay a message to the prisoner. The prison administration will decide whether to pass the information along to the inmate.

Prisoners can make phone calls based on their legal status:

- Untried prisoners must request authorization from the judicial authority.
- Convicted prisoners are generally allowed to contact family members, though this right can be revoked. For other calls, authorization from the head of the establishment is required.

Requests for phone calls must be made in writing, including details such as names and contact information. Phone access policies vary by facility. Calls are at the inmate's expense and may be monitored by the prison administration. The use of mobile phones and internet communication is prohibited.

Prisoner Outreach

Prisoner outreach initiatives in France play a critical role in addressing the challenges faced by incarcerated individuals and facilitating their re-integration into society. Organizations such as *Fondation de France* and *Wake Up Café* focus on improving inmates' educational and vocational skills, which is essential given that about 63% of released prisoners re-offend within five years due to inadequate support and opportunities. These outreach programs often provide services that include personalized support for housing, employment, and healthcare, aiming to break the cycle of recidivism. Moreover, these initiatives emphasize the importance of maintaining social ties through family visits and communication, recognizing that emotional support is pivotal for the mental well-being of inmates.[67] Additionally, the French penal system increasingly promotes alternative sentences and community service as effective means of rehabilitation, which dovetails with outreach efforts to create connections between prisoners and community resources.

Prison Scams

Scammers often target the families and friends of U.S. prisoners in France, exploiting the emotional distress caused by incarceration to manipulate victims into sending money or personal information. These scams typically involve fraudsters pretending to be inmates or their legal representatives, creating fabricated stories about legal issues to generate a sense of urgency. Victims, believing they are helping their loved ones, end up losing significant amounts of money, often through untraceable payment methods.

Families should be cautious of urgent requests, such as claims for bail or medical emergencies, and should be particularly wary of demands for payment through unusual channels like gift cards or cryptocurrency, as legitimate authorities never request payments in these ways. If the scammer knows detailed personal information about the inmate or the family,

---

67   https://pfi.org/where-we-work/europe/france

this could be a sign of a more sophisticated fraud operation, requiring thorough verification before proceeding with any financial transactions.

If you suspect a scam, stop all communication immediately and refrain from providing any more personal or financial information. Contact your bank or credit card company to secure your accounts and consider placing a fraud alert on your credit file. It's also important to document the details of the scam and report it to law enforcement, as well as agencies like the *Internet Crime Complaint Center* (IC3), to help prevent further fraud.

 **Law of the Land Hypothetical**

HYPOTHETICAL: *Your friend Dan has been arrested in Paris, and while you live in New York, you're one of the few people he can rely on. Dan doesn't have close family, so you want to reach out to him by phone to understand what happened and send him some money to help make his situation a bit more bearable. What can you do?*

ANSWER: *First, reach out to the American Embassy in Paris for assistance. They can help facilitate communication and provide information about Dan's situation. To inquire about making a phone call to Dan, contact the police station where he is being held. The embassy can also visit him to ensure his safety and well-being. To send money, you can use international transfer services such as MoneyGram or Western Union. The embassy can assist with the transfer and may also provide a list of English-speaking local attorneys. It's important for Dan to hire a lawyer to ensure he has the appropriate legal representation.*

CHAPTER 13
THE ADMINISTRATION OF JUSTICE

CHAPTER 13

THE ADMINISTRATION
OF JUSTICE

France's Legal System

The primary sources of law in France are statutory laws, particularly those codified within major legal codes such as the Civil Code (*Code Civil*), Penal Code (*Code Pénal*), and Commercial Code (*Code de Commerce*). These codes provide comprehensive frameworks for civil, criminal, and commercial matters, while also embodying the fundamental principles of French law—principles like clarity, accessibility, and legal certainty.

France operates under a dual legal system, distinguishing between public law (*droit public*), which governs the relationship between individuals and the state, and private law (*droit privé*), which regulates interactions among private individuals. Key principles such as legality and equality before the law are fundamental to the French legal framework, ensuring laws are applied uniformly and without discrimination. Additionally, the Constitution of the Fifth Republic, enacted in 1958, serves as the foundational document that outlines the structure and function of the state, safeguarding individual rights and liberties against potential government overreach.

The French legal system is organized into two primary branches: the judiciary and the administrative hierarchy. The judiciary handles civil and criminal matters through the ordinary courts (*ordre judiciaire*), while administrative courts (*ordre administratif*) deal with disputes involving public authorities. This dual system ensures that legal matters are addressed by specialized courts according to their nature, with each system operating independently.

The standard legal procedure in France is governed by the Civil Procedure Code, encompassing several key stages that ensure due process in civil litigation. Proceedings typically begin with the filing of a writ of summons, which must specify the claims and supporting evidence. Parties are required to attempt amicable resolution before initiating court actions, especially in cases involving smaller claims. After the initial claim, a structured instruction phase (*mise en état*) follows, during which both parties exchange evidence and arguments under judicial oversight. Once the case is deemed ready, a hearing is scheduled where oral pleadings occur, and the judge issues a judgment based on the presented facts and legal arguments. Appeals can be filed against decisions rendered by lower courts, allowing for a thorough review of the legal aspects of the case by higher courts, including the Court of Cassation, which focuses solely on matters of law rather than factual determinations.[68]

 **France's Judiciary**

The judiciary's primary function is to interpret and apply the law impartially and fairly, ensuring that justice is served for all individuals. Judges are tasked with hearing cases, assessing evidence, and making rulings based on the principles set forth in the Civil Code, Penal Code, and other statutory laws. This role reinforces the concept of legal certainty and predictability in the application of laws, as citizens are entitled to know their rights and obligations under the law.

Additionally, the judiciary serves as a key mechanism for safeguarding individual rights and freedoms, as enshrined in the Constitution and various international human rights treaties to which France is a party. Through judicial review, courts have the authority to examine the

---

68 https://www.lexology.com/library/detail.
aspx?g=d3a807af-8b52-4940-a899-64c2e7249f4b

constitutionality of laws and government actions, thereby acting as a check on power and preventing any potential abuses or violations of fundamental rights.

The French judicial system is divided into two main branches: the judicial courts, which handle criminal and civil matters, and the administrative courts, which deal with public law. The highest court in the judicial system is the Supreme Court of Appeals (*Cour de cassation*), followed by 36 courts of appeal, 161 *tribunaux de grande instance* (regional courts), and 307 *tribunaux d'instance* (the lowest level of courts).

At the top of the administrative courts is the Council of State (*Conseil d'État*), which oversees administrative law. The administrative branch also includes eight courts of appeal (*cours administratives d'appel*) and 42 *tribunaux administratifs*.

A unique feature of the French judiciary is the Constitutional Council (*Conseil constitutionnel*). This body reviews proposed laws for constitutionality before they are enacted, monitors national elections, and addresses questions from citizens about the constitutionality of laws. The Conseil constitutionnel is composed of nine members: three appointed by the president, three by the head of the National Assembly, and three by the head of the Senate.

Each court in the French legal system has a distinct role in adjudicating disputes, ensuring justice, and upholding the rule of law:

- **Local courts** *(tribunaux d'instance)* handle minor civil and criminal cases, offering essential access to justice for ordinary citizens.

- **Courts of appeal** *(cour d'appel)* review decisions made by lower courts to ensure that legal standards are consistently applied and to correct any errors in law.

- **The Court of Cassation** oversees legal consistency across the judiciary, focusing on ensuring that laws are correctly interpreted and applied, but without revisiting the factual aspects of cases.

- In administrative law, the **Council of State** acts as a check on government actions, ruling on the legality of administrative decisions and ensuring that public authorities act within the boundaries of the law.

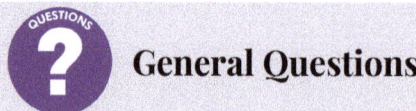 **General Questions**

1. *Will the court treat first-time offenders and tourists with more leniency?* The French judiciary often extends leniency towards first-time offenders, emphasizing rehabilitation over punishment through alternative sanctions like community service or probation.[69] Similarly, tourists are treated with understanding, especially for minor offenses, as the courts recognize cultural differences and aim to foster goodwill, which reflects an approach that values societal reintegration and positive international relations.

2. *If I am charged with a crime, which court is likely to hear my case?* If you are charged with a crime in France, the court that is likely to hear your case depends on the severity of the offense. For minor offenses (*contraventions*), the Police Court (*tribunal de police*) will preside over the case. For less serious felonies (*délits*), the Correctional Court (*tribunal correctionnel*) will be responsible, while serious crimes (*crimes*) will be adjudicated by the Assize Court (*cour d'assises*).

---

69 https://www.journals.uchicago.edu/doi/10.1086/685538

3. ***What is the standard of proof in a criminal case in France?***
In criminal cases in France, the standard of proof is based on the principle of "innermost belief" (*conviction intime*), which requires that the judges must be convinced of the defendant's guilt to a sufficient degree before rendering a conviction.[70] This standard emphasizes the necessity for the prosecution to establish the defendant's guilt beyond a reasonable doubt, ensuring a strong safeguard for the presumption of innocence throughout the judicial process.

Takeaways

- **Codified Legal Framework:** France's legal system is based on statutory laws, particularly the Civil Code, Penal Code, and Commercial Code, which provide comprehensive frameworks for civil, criminal, and commercial matters. These codes ensure clarity, accessibility, and legal certainty.

- **Dual Legal System:** France has a dual legal system distinguishing between public law (*droit public*), which governs the relationship between individuals and the state, and private law (*droit privé*), which regulates interactions between private individuals.

- **Judiciary Structure and Branches:** The judiciary is divided into two branches: judicial courts (handling civil and criminal matters) and administrative courts (dealing with public law issues). The highest judicial authority is the Court of Cassation, and the highest administrative authority is the Council of State (*Conseil d'État*).

- **Court Procedures:** Civil procedures follow a structured process under the Civil Procedure Code, beginning with a writ of summons, followed by an evidence exchange, and concluding with a

---

70 https://news.bloomberglaw.com/white-collar-and-criminal-law/insight-french-criminal-procedures-surprising-features-of-a-french-trial

hearing and judgment. Appeals can be made to higher courts, such as the Court of Cassation, for legal review.

- **Role of the Constitutional Council:** The Constitutional Council (*Conseil constitutionnel*) plays a key role in reviewing laws for constitutionality, monitoring elections, and addressing citizen questions about the constitutionality of laws before they are enacted.

 **Law of the Land Hypothetical**

HYPOTHETICAL: *Jack is an American tourist and is visiting Paris for the first time. While walking back to his hotel one evening, he unknowingly passes by a site where a crime has just occurred. The police in their search for suspects have detained Jack because he matches the general description of the perpetrator. Despite Jack's protests of innocence, he is taken into custody and charged with theft. He is unable to communicate with the officers as he does not speak French, and they do not speak English. What should Jack do?*

ANSWER: *Once Jack is detained and informed of his rights, he should request contact with the U.S. Embassy, which will provide him with a list of English-speaking attorneys to ensure his fair treatment. While his lawyer works to gather evidence and prove his innocence, Jack should fully cooperate with the police investigation. His case highlights the vital importance of consular assistance, skilled legal representation, and a thorough defense when navigating the justice system of a foreign country. While his rights are protected through the support of his lawyer and the U.S. Embassy, it is essential that John understands and cooperates with the French legal system.*

CRIME VICTIM ASSISTANCE

CRIME VICTIM ASSISTANCE

 ## Overview

In France, victims of crime have access to a comprehensive support system, including a network of organizations that provide emotional, psychological, and legal assistance.

France Victimes is a key umbrella organization offering counseling and legal support, as well as information on victims' rights. They also provide referrals to other services and can help with legal advice. Their staff includes English-speaking counselors. You can reach them at 116-006 (or +33 1 80 52 33 76 from the U.S.) from 9 AM to 7 PM (local time), or by email at victimes@france-victimes.fr.

Victims in France are also eligible for financial assistance programs, including the *Guarantee Fund for Victims* (FGTI), which compensates for medical expenses and living costs related to the crime. Additionally, victims who meet certain financial criteria are entitled to free legal aid, ensuring access to legal counsel in the judicial process. Specialized services are available for vulnerable groups, such as women facing domestic violence and child victims.

In Paris, *Paris Aide Aux Victimes* offers legal advice and support at two locations:

- 4-14 rue Ferrus, 75014 Paris (Tel: 01-4588-1800)
- 22 rue Jacques Kellner, 75017 Paris (Tel: 01-5306-8350)

They can also be contacted at contact13@pav75.fr. While these organizations are not a substitute for legal counsel, they provide valuable guidance and can refer victims to qualified attorneys.

What to Do If You Are the Victim of a Crime

If you're a victim of a crime in France, start by reporting the crime in person at the nearest police station. Provide detailed information, including evidence like medical certificates or bills. You can file a **simple complaint** or a **complaint with civil party status** to seek compensation and participate in the legal process.

Next, contact your country's embassy for consular assistance. They can connect you with victims' organizations like *France Victimes*, which offer legal support and guidance. Although these organizations can help you prepare your claim, you'll need a lawyer to submit it and navigate the legal process. Lawyers' fees are your responsibility but may be covered by compensation or legal aid. The U.S. Embassy can provide a list of English-speaking lawyers.

Keep records of damages, such as medical expenses, and claim civil party status if you haven't done so already. Retain travel documents (passport stamps, tickets, etc.) to prove you were legally in France.

The legal process can take weeks or months, though minor cases may be resolved quicker. Your lawyer can represent you while you're abroad, but you may need to testify in court.

Victim Compensation in France

Under French law, all victims of crimes committed on French soil are eligible for compensation, provided they are legally in France, whether as a tourist or a resident. Victims' compensation is determined by commissions known as *Commissions d'indemnisation des victimes d'infractions* (CIVI), located at each Tribunal de Grande Instance. These commissions assess both material and non-material damages, including psychological, emotional, and income-related losses. Compensation may also cover legal costs, including travel expenses related to the legal process.

While victims' assistance organizations can help you prepare an initial claim, hiring a lawyer is recommended to navigate the bureaucracy and avoid procedural mistakes. To recover damages, French law generally addresses compensation through the perpetrator (if identified) and the victim's insurance. However, when these sources are unavailable, a state fund, the *Fonds de Garantie*, provides compensation. This fund primarily covers serious crimes, such as wrongful death, severe personal injury (causing at least one month of lost activity or long-term effects), and sexual violence, but offers limited compensation for other types of crime.

 **Common Financial Scams in France**

In France, several financial scams pose significant threats to consumers, particularly as the digital world evolves. Common scams include pickpocketing in crowded tourist areas, fraudulent currency exchange booths that offer unfavorable rates, and scams involving fake tickets for attractions.[71] Additionally, the "gold ring scam," where scammers offer a found ring to passersby and then demand money for it, remains prevalent).

Online shopping scams, such as counterfeit goods and non-delivery schemes, have surged with the rise in e-commerce, misleading consumers into making purchases from fraudulent sites.[72] Moreover, identity theft and phishing attempts, often delivered through text messages and emails, exploit personal information for financial gain.

Sexual Assault

If you are a victim of sexual assault in France, it is crucial to prioritize your safety and well-being. First, seek immediate medical attention at the nearest hospital or emergency room, where you can receive care for any injuries and have the option for a forensic examination. To report the incident, you can go directly to a police station (commissariat de police) or contact the emergency services by calling **17** or **112**, where trained officers can assist you. If you prefer a more confidential approach, the French government provides a free online chat service with national police available 24/7 for guidance on reporting options and support resources.

---

71 https://blog.avast.com/paris-scams

72 https://www.bitdefender.com/en-us/blog/hotforsecurity/1-in-10-consumers-in-france-are-targeted-by-scammers-fraud-losses-of-5-9-billion-take-victims-on-an-emotional-rollercoaster-says-gasa

As a victim of sexual assault in France, you have a range of legal rights designed to protect and support you throughout the judicial process. You have the right to receive information about your rights and the legal proceedings, including access to medical and psychological support services. Victims are entitled to assistance from victim support organizations (such as *France Victimes*, *SOS Femmes*, and *Le Comité des Femmes*), which provide guidance and emotional support. Moreover, you have the right to legal representation and may qualify for legal aid, ensuring that you can navigate the justice system effectively. The French legal system also recognizes the importance of confidentiality, protecting your identity during investigations and trials to uphold your dignity and privacy.[73]

Consular Assistance

U.S. embassies and consulates offer essential support to victims of crime abroad by addressing emergency needs arising from the incident and facilitating access to appropriate medical care. They provide guidance on how to report the crime to local law enforcement and may accompany victims to the police station when possible. Additionally, they assist in obtaining updates about the legal case from local authorities and help replace lost or stolen passports.

Embassies also connect victims with resources both overseas and in the U.S., explain financial assistance options for returning home, and assist with travel arrangements. They can contact designated individuals in the U.S. while adhering to privacy regulations.

The resources available can vary by location, but the nearest U.S. embassy or consulate can provide information about local doctors, counselors, and legal professionals to help victims after a crime. Timely medical treatment is crucial, particularly after certain incidents. The embassy can inform you about medical options and associated costs in the host country, including care for sexually transmitted infections or unwanted pregnancies. In serious cases like sexual assault, a forensic exam may be

---

73 https://victim-support.eu/infovictims-france

necessary to collect evidence for prosecution, ideally conducted within 72 hours after the incident.

However, keep in mind the U.S. embassy or consulate does not cover legal, medical, or other expenses for victims of crime. Additionally, consular officers are unable to investigate crimes, offer legal advice, or act as official interpreters or translators.[74]

 **Safety Tips**

- Be mindful of your surroundings and avoid distractions like excessive phone use.
- If something feels wrong or makes you uncomfortable, leave the situation.
- Whenever possible, go out with friends or trusted individuals.
- Choose reputable taxis or rideshare services instead of accepting rides from strangers.
- Be aware of your alcohol and substance consumption to maintain control over your situation.
- Communicate your boundaries assertively and be firm if someone crosses them.
- Familiarize yourself with local emergency numbers and resources available for support.
- Know safe places you can go and have a plan for how to get there if needed.

---

74 https://travel.state.gov/content/dam/NEWTravelAssets/pdfs/Crime%20 Victim%20Assistance_Brochure

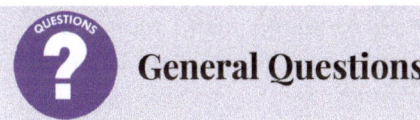

General Questions

1. *If I am a victim of a crime, can I legally be compensated?* **Yes**. To claim compensation for damages, victims can file through the Commission for the Compensation of Victims of Crime (CIVI) at each Tribunal de Grande Instance. A lawyer or France Victimes can assist with the process. To apply, send a registered letter or deliver it to the CIVI office, including your name, birth details, occupation, nationality, address, and ID copy. If you're not the victim, provide proof of your relationship. Include details of the crime (date, place, circumstances), police reports, trial information, and judgments. Submit a list of damages, such as medical bills, lost wages, and emotional harm, with supporting documents. Also, provide compensation received from insurance, the offender, or other sources, along with your financial details and bank account information.

2. *If a family member falls victim to homicide, can I bring the body back to my home country?* **Yes**, if a family member falls victim to homicide in France, you can repatriate the body to your home country. However, you must follow legal procedures involving local authorities, obtain necessary documentation, and potentially navigate the complexities of ongoing investigations (**https://www.connexionfrance.com/news/2024-rules-for-re-patriating-a-body-to-or-from-france/682711**). It is advisable to work with a funeral director experienced in international repatriation to ensure compliance with both French regulations and the requirements of your home country. Additionally, you may need to consult the consulate of your home country for assistance during this process.

3. *If a family member falls victim to homicide, will I receive any assistance from the French government?* **Yes**, if a family member falls victim to homicide in France, you may receive assistance from the French government. This includes emotional and psychological support through victim support organizations such as France Victimes, which offer free services to victims' families. Additionally, you may also be eligible for financial compensation through the Guarantee Fund for Victims (FGTI), which provides support for funeral expenses and other costs related to the loss. The government recognizes the need to aid families during such traumatic events, ensuring access to necessary resources and support.

CHAPTER 15
POLICE

CHAPTER 15

POLICE

Overview[75]

In France, there are three primary police forces: the *Police Nationale*, the *Gendarmerie Nationale*, and the *Compagnie Républicaine de la Sécurité* (CRS). The Police Nationale, under the Interior Ministry, manages urban crime and is identifiable by officers in silver-buttoned uniforms. They often wear white caps and capes in adverse conditions. The Gendarmerie Nationale functions as part of the military under the Ministry of Defense, wearing blue uniforms with gold buttons, focusing on serious crime and rural law enforcement, including motorway patrols and air safety. Lastly, the CRS, known as the riot police, is primarily responsible for crowd control and public disturbances but also performs lifesaving duties during summer. Together, these forces form a comprehensive structure for maintaining public safety across urban and rural areas in France.

As of 2023, the French police force comprises approximately 245,000 personnel, including both the Police Nationale and Gendarmerie Nationale. Despite this significant number, many reports indicate that the force is not adequately staffed to meet the demands of public safety, with ongoing concerns about high workloads, insufficient personnel in certain regions, and challenges such as increasing crime rates and public

---

75 https://www.justlanded.com/english/France/Articles/Culture/
The-French-police

disturbances.[76] Consequently, the staffing levels remain a contentious issue, highlighting the need for further recruitment and support to enhance the effectiveness of law enforcement in France.

 ## Police Response

The French police perform various essential functions aimed at maintaining public safety and enforcing the law. The core responsibilities of the police include conducting investigations into criminal activities, managing public order during demonstrations and events, and ensuring traffic safety on roads and highways. The Police Nationale primarily operates in urban areas and focuses on addressing everyday crimes, while the Gendarmerie Nationale, which also serves rural regions, handles serious offenses on a national scale. Another critical function is the prevention of crime, which involves community engagement initiatives that foster collaboration between law enforcement and citizens to enhance public trust and reduce criminal activity. Additionally, specialized units within the police are responsible for specific tasks such as counter-terrorism efforts, cybercrime prevention, and assistance in emergency situations, including search and rescue operations.

The French police force operates at three key levels: federal, state, and municipal, each with distinct responsibilities. At the federal level, the Police Nationale and Gendarmerie Nationale are the primary agencies, with the former overseeing urban policing and the latter focusing on rural areas and national security tasks. The Gendarmerie also manages highway patrol and serious crime investigations. At the state level, law enforcement is coordinated through departmental and regional divisions under the authority of a Préfet, who ensures collaboration between the Police Nationale and Gendarmerie to address local crime. Municipally, local police forces, called *police municipale*, operate under the mayor's jurisdiction, handling public order, minor offenses, and

---

76 https://www.statista.com/topics/11212/police-in-france/

community issues. In larger cities, specialized units within the *Préfecture de Police* provide additional urban security functions. This multi-layered structure enables a tailored approach to policing, catering to the diverse needs of communities across France.

Police and Community Relations

The general reputation of the French police is mixed, characterized by both public support and significant criticism. While some citizens view the police as essential for maintaining public order and safety, there is a growing perception of systemic issues, particularly concerning excessive use of force and racial profiling, especially toward minority communities. High-profile incidents of police violence, such as those during protests, have sparked widespread outrage and calls for reform, leading to a heightened mistrust among certain demographics. Surveys indicate fluctuating levels of trust in the police, with recent data showing that approximately 70% of the population expressed trust in the police in early 2024, though this figure masks deeper societal divisions regarding police practices.[77]

In 2022, the *Inspection Générale de la Police Nationale* (IGPN) launched investigations into 51 incidents of disproportionate force and failures to protect arrested individuals. Observers note that French police tend to be more heavily armed than their European counterparts, utilizing weapons that might be banned or seldom deployed elsewhere. Reports from Amnesty International highlight various allegations of human rights violations committed by law enforcement officials. Additionally, systemic racism has been a pressing concern, with the *UN Committee on the Elimination of Racial Discrimination* (CERD) expressing alarm over the aggressive tactics used against minority groups. Public misconduct incidents, such as a widely circulated audio clip in March 2023 showing police officers employing excessive force during protests, have further fueled the controversy.

---

77 https://www.statista.com/statistics/1004491/
    trust-level-national-police-france

Police Use of Force

In France, the issue of police use of force has grown increasingly significant, especially in recent years. Tensions between law enforcement and certain communities, particularly in urban areas with high immigrant populations or marginalized groups, have reached a boiling point. These tensions have sparked widespread concern about the conduct of police officers and raised allegations of excessive use of force, especially during moments of unrest such as protests, riots, or police interventions in poorer neighborhoods.

Critics of the police often highlight disproportionate force as a major issue. In numerous instances, they argue, police have used excessive tactics against racial minorities, young people, and protesters. The deployment of baton charges, rubber bullets, and even chokeholds has raised alarms for being excessively aggressive, especially in situations where alternative, less violent methods could have been employed.

Compounding this concern is the issue of **racial profiling and discrimination.** Young men of North African or Sub-Saharan African descent are often singled out by police, an issue that has long plagued France. This kind of profiling only deepens the divide between law enforcement and certain communities, perpetuating a cycle of mistrust and resentment. Many argue that this systemic racism within the police exacerbates the already tense relationship between law enforcement and marginalized groups.

Furthermore, a significant number of critics argue that there is a **lack of accountability** when it comes to police actions. Despite numerous incidents of excessive force, many believe that officers are not adequately held responsible for their actions. There are widespread accusations of insufficient transparency in police investigations and legal proceedings. Activists often claim that police unions protect officers from facing real consequences, thereby shielding them from punishment even in the face of serious misconduct. This lack of accountability has contributed to a sense of impunity within the police force and a perception that justice is often not served when abuses occur.

In recent years, France has introduced reforms to address concerns about police use of force, though many believe deeper issues remain. The controversial chokehold technique was banned in 2020 to reduce excessive force, and body cameras were rolled out to increase transparency. Efforts to strengthen police oversight, including calls for greater independence of the General Inspectorate of the National Police (IGPN), have been made. Following the Yellow Vest protests, guidelines on the use of force and crowd control tactics were revised, but critics argue these changes are insufficient. The 2020 **Global Security Law**, which expanded police surveillance, sparked protests over restrictions on filming police, leading to amendments but leaving broader concerns about police authority unresolved.[78] While these reforms are steps forward, many activists call for more systemic changes to address police violence, racism, and accountability.

 ## General Questions

1. *What do French police say when arresting someone in France?*
   The French police typically say "*Vous êtes en état d'arrestation*" when arresting someone in France, which translates to "You are under arrest" in English. [79]

---

78 https://www.publicinternationallawandpoli-
    cygroup.org/lawyering-justice-blog/2020/12/13/
    frances-global-security-law-article-24-and-the-right-to-information

79 https://brainly.com/question/39005352

2. *Is it legal to take videos of the French police?* **Yes**, it is generally legal to take videos of French police officers in public spaces, as long as the filming is done for lawful purposes. However, recent laws have introduced restrictions on sharing images of police officers if there is intent to harm or identify them, particularly if it poses a threat to their physical or psychological integrity. This legislation has raised concerns regarding press freedom and the ability to document police activities, especially during protests or demonstrations. Therefore, while filming is legal, the context and intent behind sharing those images must be carefully considered to avoid legal repercussions.[80]

Law of the Land True Story[81]

On December 6, 1986, Malik Oussekine tragically found himself near student protests in Paris opposing changes to the university admission system and the introduction of tuition fees. During the police's crackdown on the demonstrators, Oussekine was reportedly chased into a building and violently beaten with batons. An ambulance was summoned, but he was pronounced dead shortly after arriving at the hospital. The French public prosecutor later claimed that the injuries Oussekine sustained were not severe enough to have caused his death and attributed it to a heart attack. His death sparked riots in Paris, prompting national reflection, especially after it was revealed he had actually died in the hallway where the police attacked him. In January 1990, two officers, Jean Schmitt and Christophe Garcia, faced charges related to his death but ultimately received only suspended prison sentences.

---

80 https://www.justiceinitiative.org/voices/
caught-film-what-law-says-about-filming-police-europe

81 https://www.bbc.com/culture/
article/20220510-the-police-killing-that-shocked-france

HOW TO GET LEGAL HELP IN FRANCE

HOW TO GET LEGAL
HELP IN FRANCE

 **Available Resources**

If you find yourself in legal trouble as a visitor in France, there are several resources available to assist you. First, the French legal system allows foreign visitors to access legal aid services, which can help cover the costs of legal representation and guidance. Organizations such as *Les Points d'accès au Droit* and *Maisons de Justice et du Droit* provide free legal consultations and assistance in various cities across France. These resources cater to individuals facing issues ranging from civil disputes to criminal allegations, ensuring that visitors can receive adequate support.[82]

Another prominent option is the Point-Justice system, created in December 2020, which consists of dedicated legal information points throughout the country. With around 2,000 locations marked by a distinct green logo, these points provide free and confidential legal advice from professionals, including lawyers and mediators. Typically, legal experts are available at these points for limited hours, so it is recommended

---

82 https://www.service-public.fr/particuliers/vosdroits/F18074?lang=en

to make appointments in advance, especially if you need advice on topics such as housing, family, or employment issues. For your nearest Point-Justice location, you can search online or call the free number 3039 from mainland France.

 **http://www.annuaires.justice.gouv.fr/annuaires-12162/ les-point-justice-34055.html**

In addition, each department in France has a *Conseil départemental de l'accès au droit* (CDAD), which aims to ensure that everyone has access to legal assistance. These councils organize appointments where legal experts can explain visitors' rights, advise on eligibility for legal aid, and recommend relevant associations that may offer further help.

 **https://consultation.avocat.fr/les-avocats-tout-savoir/ consultations-gratuites-avocat.html**

For those living in rural areas without easy access to a Point-Justice, local *mairies* (town halls) can also provide information and support. You can find the contact details and address for your local mairie at **https:// lannuaire.service-public.fr/**

Additionally, certain consumer associations offer their members free legal consultations, thereby expanding the available assistance networks for foreign visitors dealing with legal matters in France. Furthermore, organizations like *Avocats au service des victimes* focus on assisting foreigners and victims of crime, offering essential legal advice and support during difficult circumstances.

Legal Aid

Foreign visitors in France facing legal issues are eligible for legal aid, provided they meet specific financial criteria established by the French legal system. This legal support is extended to all individuals regardless of nationality, reflecting a commitment to equality under the law. To qualify, applicants must demonstrate inadequate financial resources to cover their legal costs.[83] The evaluation process considers the applicant's income and wealth, potentially granting full or partial legal aid based on these factors.

Legal aid encompasses various types of legal matters, including civil disputes, criminal cases, and administrative issues. Unique provisions allow victims of criminal acts or domestic violence to access aid without financial assessment, highlighting France's focus on supporting vulnerable individuals in need.

The application process for legal aid involves submitting a *cerfa* form, which requires documentation to verify identity, residency, and financial status. The legal aid office reviews applications to determine eligibility based on the applicant's circumstances and financial condition.

 ## Foreign Embassies in France

When individuals find themselves in legal trouble while traveling or residing in a foreign country, the role of their home embassy or consulate becomes crucial. These diplomatic missions provide essential support and assistance to their citizens, ensuring that they have access to necessary resources and guidance during challenging legal situations.

One of the primary roles of an embassy or consulate in situations of legal trouble is to provide vital information and resources to citizens. Upon notification of a citizen's legal difficulties, embassies typically offer guidance about local legal systems, including information about the local judicial process and rights of the detained individual. This information is critical, as legal frameworks can vary significantly from one country to another.

---

83 https://www.service-public.fr/particuliers/vosdroits/F18074?lang=en

Embassies can inform individuals about governmental and NGO resources that may provide further support, reflecting their commitment to ensuring that their citizens possess the tools needed to deal with legal matters. They also maintain lists of local attorneys who speak the language of the detainee and are familiar with the local legal system, thus offering direct assistance in securing legal representation.

Paris hosts 159 embassies; in addition, there are 482 consulates and four other representations in France. Below are just a few of the foreign embassies. For a full list, please visit **https://www.embassypages.com/ france**

U.S. Embassy

2 avenue Gabriel
75382 Paris Cedex 08
France
Tel: (+33) 1 43.12.22.22
Website: fr.usembassy.gov

Canadian Embassy

130 rue du Faubourg saint-Honoré
Paris 75008
France
Tel: (+33) (0) 1 44 43 29 00
Website: www.canadainternational.gc.ca/france/

Brazilian Embassy

34, cours Albert 1er
75008 Paris
France
Tel: (+1 809) 532-4200
Website: paris.itamaraty.gov.br

British Embassy

35 rue du Faubourg St Honoré
75383 Paris Cedex 08

France
Tel: (+33) 1 44 51 31 00
Website: www.gov.uk/government/world/france

Italian Embassy

Varenne street 51
75007 Paris
France
Tel: (+33) 1 49 54 03 00
Website: www.ambparigi.esteri.it

German Embassy

24 rue Marbeau
BP 30 221
75116 Paris
France
Tel: (+33) 1 53 83 45 00
Website: www.paris.diplo.de

 **General Questions**

1. *Is legal aid available to tourist in France?* **Yes**. If you are a foreigner who is not a resident of France, you can acquire the legal aid form from the central authority your country has appointed to handle international legal aid applications. In most cases, this designated authority is the Ministry of Justice in your country.[84]

---

84 https://e-justice.europa.eu/37129/FR/legal_aid?FRANCE&clang=en#:~:-text=If%20you%20are%20a%20foreigner,transmit%20international%20legal%20aid%20applications.

2. ***Can a recipient of legal aid choose his lawyer?*** **Yes.** As a recipient of legal aid, you have the right to choose your lawyer and any law clerk to support you in your legal proceedings. This selection can be made at the beginning of the process, even prior to the court's decision to grant you legal aid. However, it is essential to note that the lawyer has the discretion to accept or decline your request for assistance.[85]

---

85 https://www.service-public.fr/particuliers/vosdroits/F18074?lang=en

MEDICAL FACILITIES & HOSPITALS

MEDICAL FACILITIES & HOSPITALS

Overview[86]

The overall standard of the healthcare system in France is notably high, characterized by a comprehensive public insurance scheme known as *Protection Maladie Universelle* (PUMA), which covers about 96% of residents, including expatriates after a residency period. France's system is renowned for its efficient delivery of healthcare services, minimal wait times for appointments, and accessibility to high-quality care, including preventative services such as free medical checkups every two years.[87]

The majority of hospitals are state-owned and not-for-profit, promoting excellent medical standards and regular health maintenance for the population. Additionally, the integration of alternative therapies under public insurance highlights the system's holistic approach to health. While funded by significant taxes, the French healthcare system manages to provide extensive care to all legal residents, regardless of employment status, although expatriates must initially secure private insurance until they become eligible for public coverage. Consequently, the French

---

86 https://www.internationalinsurance.com/health/systems/france.php?utm_source=google&utm_medium=cpc&utm_campaign=US-Dynamic&gad_source=1&gclid=EAIaIQobChMIvveFz_esigMV64FaB-R14cyEbEAAYASAAEgIv0_D_BwE

87 https://www.who.int/news/item/07-02-2000-world-health-organization-assesses-the-world's-health-systems

healthcare system stands as one of the leading models globally, balancing universal access, high-quality service, and a commitment to public health outcomes.

Visitors' Access to Healthcare in France

Visitors to France can access medical services through several avenues, ensuring that their healthcare needs are met during their stay. The country's healthcare system is robust and provides various options for tourists and short-term residents. While the French healthcare system, PUMA, primarily caters to residents, visitors can nonetheless access essential medical services. Tourists from European Economic Area (EEA) countries can utilize their European Health Insurance Card (EHIC) to receive necessary healthcare services at reduced costs or free of charge during their stay in France.[88] For visitors from outside the EEA, it is advisable to obtain travel health insurance that covers medical expenses incurred during their visit, as this insurance can facilitate access to private healthcare providers and reimburse applicable costs.

In emergencies, all visitors, irrespective of their insurance status, have the right to receive immediate medical attention, including treatment at hospitals and clinics.[89] Therefore, individuals should be aware of how to access local medical facilities when needed.

Types of Medical Services Available

Medical services in France encompass a broad range of healthcare provisions, including general practitioner visits, hospital care, specialists, and emergency services. Visitors can easily find a general practitioner (*médecin généraliste*) for routine medical consultations and can also refer patients to specialists if needed. Pharmacies, which are ubiquitous

---

88 https://www.expatica.com/fr/healthcare/
     healthcare-basics/a-guide-to-the-french-healthcare-system-101166/

89 https://washington.consulfrance.org/
     health-pass-what-to-know-if-you-are-traveling-to-france

throughout France, can also assist visitors with minor ailments and offer advice on over-the-counter medications.

In cases of severe medical concerns or emergencies, visitors can access hospital services, or the urgent care (*urgences*) provided by public hospitals. It is essential to call the emergency number **112** for urgent medical care, which ensures swift attention from emergency medical services.

One major barrier for visitors is the language barrier when seeking medical services. Language barriers significantly impede access to medical care in France, leading to misunderstandings that can result in misdiagnosis and inappropriate treatment. These barriers also prevent patients from effectively communicating their health concerns and adhering to treatment plans, thereby negatively impacting health outcomes. While France has implemented interpretation services to mitigate these challenges, greater integration and training for healthcare providers are essential to ensure equitable access to care for non-French speaking patients.

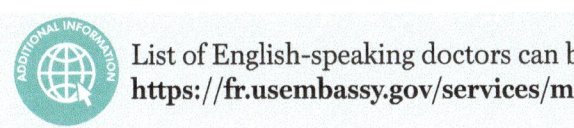

List of English-speaking doctors can be found at
https://fr.usembassy.gov/services/medical-assistance/

Hospitals and International Medical Facilities

As of 2021, there were approximately 2,987 hospitals in France, providing a mix of public and private healthcare services to the population.[90] In terms of medical staff, France has around 1.1 million healthcare professionals, including approximately 764,000 nurses, 336,000 doctors, and a notable number of other medical personnel, ensuring comprehensive healthcare coverage across the nation.[91]

---

90 https://www.statista.com/statistics/557012/hospitals-in-france/

91 https://healthsystemsfacts.org/france/france-health-system-personnel

Hospitals in France are predominantly concentrated in urban areas, particularly in major cities such as Paris, Lyon, Marseille, and Lille, where the population density is higher, and healthcare needs are more pronounced. This urban concentration allows for better access to specialized medical services and resources. However, rural regions often have fewer hospitals, leading to disparities in healthcare access for residents outside urban centers.

France is home to several hospitals known for their exceptional reputation in healthcare delivery, research, and medical excellence. Among the top hospitals is the *Assistance Publique - Hôpitaux de Paris* (AP-HP), which is the largest hospital system in Europe and renowned for its cutting-edge clinical services and research. The *Pitié-Salpêtrière Hospital* in Paris is also highly regarded, especially for neurology and psychiatry. Additionally, the *Institut Curie* is notable for its specialized cancer treatment and research, standing as a leader in oncological care. Other esteemed institutions include the University Hospital of Toulouse and the *Centre Hospitalier Universitaire de Lille*, both recognized for their comprehensive healthcare services and innovative patient care practices, reinforcing France's position as a leader in global healthcare.

Hospitals Catering to International Visitors

France has several hospitals specifically catering to international visitors, offering services tailored to meet the needs of expatriates and tourists. *The American Hospital of Paris* is notable for its multidisciplinary approach and English-speaking staff, providing high-quality care while ensuring comfort and clear communication for non-French speakers.

The American Hospital of Paris

Address: 63 Boulevard Victor Hugo,
92200 Neuilly-sur-Seine, France
Phone: +33 (0) 1 46 41 83 76.

Additionally, hospitals like the *Institut Hospitalier Franco-Britannique* and *Hôpital Foch* also serve a significant number of international patients, offering specialized services and acceptance of various international insurances. These facilities prioritize a welcoming environment for foreign visitors, making healthcare access smoother during their stay in France.

Medical Emergencies

When faced with a medical emergency, the first step is to call the national emergency number 15, which connects you directly to the SAMU (*Services d'Aide Médicale Urgente*), the French medical emergency service. If the situation is life-threatening and requires immediate assistance, you can also call the Europe-wide emergency number 112, which functions seamlessly across European Union countries. For fire-related incidents or urgent situations requiring fire department assistance, dial 18, and 17 is the number for police emergencies.

It is essential to remain calm during the call and clearly state your emergency. Be prepared to provide vital information, such as your name, location, nature of the emergency, and any specific details about the situation, like the number of people needing help or the presence of any potential danger.

What Should You Do If You Feel Unwell in France?

If you feel unwell in France, it is important to take immediate steps to address your health concerns effectively. First, assess the severity of your symptoms; for mild issues, visiting a local pharmacy can be a good starting point, as pharmacists often provide advice and over-the-counter medications for common ailments. If your condition requires medical attention, you can schedule an appointment with a general practitioner (*médecin généraliste*), who can assess your situation and recommend further treatment if necessary. In cases of urgent or severe illness, do not hesitate to call the emergency services at **15** for SAMU or **112** for immediate assistance. It is also advisable to have your travel health insurance information handy, as it will facilitate access to healthcare services and help cover any medical expenses incurred during your visit. By following these steps, you can ensure that you receive the necessary care when feeling unwell in France.

What If You Need Hospital Care in France?

If you need hospital care while visiting France, it's important to choose the right facility for effective medical attention. Major cities like Paris, Lyon, and Marseille offer access to renowned hospitals, such as the *Pitié-Salpêtrière Hospital,* known for its comprehensive services and specialties. *The American Hospital of Paris* is particularly accommodating for international patients, providing services in English. For emergencies, call **15** for SAMU or **112** for immediate assistance, which can guide you to the nearest appropriate hospital. Regardless of location, hospitals in France must provide emergency care, and having travel health insurance will help ease access to necessary medical services and aid in cost reimbursement.

Insurance Guidance

When visiting France, understanding the nuances of health insurance coverage is vital for ensuring access to necessary medical care. Many travelers may possess the European Health Insurance Card (EHIC), which allows for coverage of medically necessary treatment during temporary stays. However, those lacking EHIC coverage should purchase travel health insurance that sufficiently covers potential medical expenses, including hospital stays, treatments, and prescription medications. Travel insurance acts as a safeguard, minimizing out-of-pocket expenses for visitors when they seek healthcare.

Moreover, securing private health insurance offers additional benefits, such as quicker access to specialists and private medical facilities, which may enhance the overall experience for those requiring non-emergency care.[92] Therefore, for peace of mind and to ensure a comprehensive safety net during their stay, visitors are strongly encouraged to assess their health insurance options before arriving in France to ensure they can access the care they may require.

---

92 https://www.expatica.com/fr/healthcare/healthcare-services/hospitals-in-france-101172/

Foreign medical insurance plans are generally accepted in France, particularly in major cities with significant expatriate populations, such as Paris. Many hospitals, especially those catering to international visitors like the American Hospital of Paris, are accustomed to working with foreign insurance providers. However, it is advisable for patients to confirm in advance whether their specific insurance plan is accepted at the facility and understand payment and reimbursement processes, which may require upfront payment for services.

As a visitor in France, you typically pay for medical services upfront, especially if you are not covered by the *European Health Insurance Card* (EHIC) or a foreign insurance plan accepted by the provider. Payments can be made using credit or debit cards, although some smaller clinics may only accept cash. After receiving care, you can submit a claim for reimbursement to your travel health insurance provider, so it's essential to keep all receipts and documentation.

For comparison purposes, according to available information, the average cost of a doctor's visit in France is around €23 (US$23.92) without coverage, but with standard health insurance, the patient typically pays only around €6.60 (US$6.87) out of pocket; an emergency room visit averages around €100 (US$103.98) without coverage and €10 (US$10.40) with coverage.

General Questions

1. *Are there English-speaking staff in French hospitals?* English-speaking healthcare options in France can vary depending on location. In Paris, expats and English-speaking visitors generally have more choices, with reputable hospitals like the *American Hospital of Paris* and *Hertford British Hospital,* where bilingual staff are available to assist in English. These hospitals are especially popular with English-speaking expats and offer a more comfortable experience for those who might not be fluent in French. However, outside of Paris, it can be much more challenging to find bilingual medical staff. While larger cities and tourist destinations may offer some bilingual services, in smaller towns and rural areas, doctors and hospital staff may not speak English fluently. In these cases, it's a good idea to bring a French-speaking companion, learn some key phrases, and use a translation app.[93]

2. *What is the average wait time to see a doctor?* Wait times for seeing a doctor in France can vary depending on the type of consultation and the treatment required. On average, from the moment you contact a doctor to the actual consultation, it typically takes about six days. However, some specialists have longer wait times. Here's an overview of average wait times for different types of doctors:

   • Pediatrician or radiologist: 3 weeks

   • Dentist: 1 month (average wait time of 17 days)

   • Gynecologist: 6 weeks (average wait time of 32 days)

   • Cardiologist: 50 days

   • Dermatologist: 2 months

   • Ophthalmologist: 80 days

---

93 https://www.internations.org/france-expats/guide/healthcare

TRUE STORY — Law of the Land True Story

A young American backpacker who injured her ankle while hiking in the Alps was able to quickly access high-quality medical care at a local clinic, despite not speaking much French. She received prompt treatment and clear communication through a helpful translation app, and the cost was manageable thanks to her travel insurance. The experience left her with a positive impression of the French healthcare system's accessibility and efficiency.

DRIVING IN FRANCE

CHAPTER 18
DRIVING IN FRANCE

Overview[94]

Driving in France is generally a smooth and efficient experience, thanks to its well-maintained road infrastructure. The country boasts a network of high-quality highways, including fast and efficient autoroutes (motorways), many of which are toll roads. In cities, roads are typically well-marked and maintained, though traffic can be dense, particularly in Paris and other major urban centers. Rural areas are connected by smaller roads, which can be narrower but are still generally in good condition. France also has a reputation for clear road signage, which is particularly helpful for foreign drivers. Parking can be challenging in city centers, but options like underground garages or paid street parking are available. While driving is straightforward, drivers should be aware of local rules and driving etiquette, including speed limits, which are strictly enforced, especially on highways and in urban areas.

 In France, most places are well connected by a range of roads, with privately-owned *autoroutes* (motorways) being the most common and typically tolled, resulting in less congestion compared to other routes. The autoroutes are clearly marked with blue signs and are numbered with an "A" prefix (e.g., A23). *Routes Nationales* (National Roads)

---

94 https://www.insurance4carhire.com/guides/driving-in-france

are usually dual carriageways and not tolled, so they can be busier. These roads are marked with green signs and an "N" prefix (e.g., N84). *Routes Départmentales* (Department Roads) are managed by local departments and are similar to National Roads but are marked with a "D" or "RD" prefix (e.g., D12). *Routes Communales* (Municipal Roads) typically connect rural areas and are single-lane roads, marked with a "C" prefix (e.g., C340). Other road-related signs to watch for include péage, indicating a toll, and bis, signaling a scenic, holiday route.

 ## Main Traffic Rules

- **Driving Side:** Vehicles drive on the right-hand side of the road in France.

- **Speed Limits:** Speed limits vary by road type, with urban areas typically allowing up to 50 km/h (31.07 miles/hour) and motorways up to 130 km/h (80.78 miles/hour).

- **Traffic Signals:** France uses a standard traffic light system, where red means stop, green allows passage, and yellow signals caution.

- **Seat Belts:** The use of seat belts is mandatory for all passengers in a vehicle, front and rear.

- **Alcohol:** The legal blood alcohol limit is 0.05 g/dL for drivers and 0.02 g/dL for novice drivers, with strict penalties for violations.

- **Mobile Devices:** Using a mobile phone while driving is prohibited unless using hands-free technology.

- **Yielding:** Drivers must yield to traffic coming from the right at intersections without signs; on roundabouts, those already in the roundabout typically have priority.

- **Toll Roads:** Many major roads in France are toll routes, and payment can be made at booths using cash or credit cards.

- **If Stopped by Police:** When stopped by police, remain calm, provide requested documents, and understand your rights.

Road Safety

Traffic accidents remain a significant concern in France, as evidenced by the rising number of fatalities and serious injuries on the roads. In 2023, approximately 3,200 road fatalities were recorded, which reflects a slight decrease from the previous year; however, the overall trend shows fluctuations that call for continued vigilance and improvement in road safety measures.[95] The increase in deaths among younger drivers and vulnerable road users, such as cyclists, highlights the importance of implementing effective safety strategies and public awareness campaigns to combat this ongoing issue. Additionally, factors such as speeding, alcohol consumption, and distracted driving continue to be prevalent causes of road accidents, necessitating a sustained focus on education and enforcement of traffic laws to enhance overall road safety in France.

To stay safe while driving in France, consider the following tips:

- **Observe Speed Limits:** Speed limits are strictly enforced, with penalties for speeding. Always pay attention to road signs, as limits can vary depending on weather conditions.

- **Drive on the Right:** In France, vehicles drive on the right side of the road. Be cautious when navigating roundabouts, which can be tricky for first-time drivers.

- **Alcohol Limits:** Avoid alcohol if you're planning to drive.

- **Parking:** Parking can be challenging in major cities, especially in central areas. Pay attention to parking signs and regulations and always park in designated areas to avoid fines.

---

95 https://www.statista.com/statistics/437904/
    number-of-road-deaths-in-france

- **Warning Triangle and Breathalyzer:** By law, you must have a warning triangle and a breathalyzer in your car. Ensure both are present before hitting the road.

- **Weather Conditions:** In the winter, especially in mountainous areas, snow chains or winter tires may be required. Check the weather forecast and prepare accordingly.

- **Roundabouts:** Yield to traffic already in the roundabout. This rule applies even if you're entering from the right.

- **Pedestrian Crossings:** Always yield to pedestrians at designated crossings, especially in cities. Pedestrian safety is a priority in France.

- **Priority Rules:** At all intersections, priority is given to traffic approaching from the right unless road signs indicate otherwise.

- **GPS:** Set up a GPS app (Apple Maps, Google Maps, Waze, etc.) for navigation before starting your journey. Use one that you're comfortable with to avoid confusion, especially in cities like Paris where street signs can be difficult to read.

Insurance and Documentation Requirements for Visitors

For foreign drivers planning to drive in France, understanding the car insurance requirements is crucial for a legal and safe driving experience. All drivers, including foreigners, must have at least third-party liability insurance, known as *"assurance responsabilité civile,"* which covers damages to third parties in the event of an accident. While it is possible for tourists to drive with insurance from their home country, the foreign insurance must meet the French minimum requirements and provide adequate coverage.[96] If you are unsure if your insurance meets France's legal minimum or leaves you with any coverage gaps, it is a good idea to speak with an insurance professional to discuss your coverage options. Foreign drivers are often required to obtain a "green card," an international insurance document that proves you have valid insurance

---

96 https://www.service-public.fr/particuliers/vosdroits/F35443?lang=en

coverage that complies with French standards. This card must be kept in the vehicle at all times for verification purposes.

In addition to insurance, foreign drivers must ensure they have the appropriate documentation before setting off on the road. A valid driver's license is essential; if the license is from a non-EU country, it is advisable to carry an International Driving Permit (IDP), which translates the license into multiple languages, facilitating easier communication with law enforcement.[97] Furthermore, it's important for foreign drivers to provide proof of vehicle registration, insurance documents, and identification, such as a passport or national ID.

Toll Roads

France's toll road system, known as *"péage,"* serves as a critical infrastructure component that facilitates efficient transportation across the country. Approximately 76% of the autoroute network consists of toll roads, which stretch over 11,882 kilometers.[98] Drivers must pay tolls based on the distance traveled and the vehicle category, which is determined by factors such as size and weight. The costs can vary significantly; for instance, typical charges range from €10 to €50 for class 1 vehicles, like standard passenger cars, depending on the specific autoroute used.[99]

Payment for tolls can be completed at designated toll booths before entering and exiting the toll sections. Various payment methods are accepted, including cash (euro coins and notes), credit and debit cards, and electronic payment systems like *"Télépéage."* The "Télépéage" system, operating through an onboard unit, allows for automatic toll payments without stopping at booths, which is convenient for frequent travelers.

97 https://frenchconnectionshcb.com/
    driving-in-france-regulations-licences-and-insurance

98 https://en.wikipedia.org/wiki/Autoroutes_of_France

99 https://www.rac.co.uk/drive/travel/
    driving-in-europe/a-complete-guide-to-toll-roads-in-france

General Questions

1. *Can I use my driver's license from my home country to drive in France?* **Yes**, you can use your home country's driver's license to drive in France. If you're from the EU/EEA, your license is valid indefinitely. If you're from a non-EU/EEA country, you can use it for up to one year after establishing residency. After that, you may need to exchange it for a French license. An International Driving Permit or translation is recommended if your license isn't in French.

2. *What is the legal minimum age to drive in France?* Minimum age for driving in France is **18** for a car and a motorcycle over 125cc, and 15 for a motorcycle under 125cc.

3. *What is the age requirement for renting a car in France?* In France, the minimum age to rent a car is generally **21 years old**. However, drivers under 25 may be subject to a young driver surcharge, typically ranging from €10 to €30 per day, depending on the rental agency and vehicle type. Additionally, most rental companies require drivers to have held a valid driver's license for at least one year. For certain car categories (e.g., luxury or high-performance vehicles), the minimum age may be higher, and some rental agencies may impose additional conditions.

Law of the Land Hypothetical

HYPOTHETICAL: Jenna and Marina are U.S. citizens. Jenna is 19 and Marina just turned 17. They are going to be vacationing in France for three weeks and want to sightsee all around the country. Upon arrival in France, the girls plan on renting a car and taking turns driving. Will Jenna and Marina encounter any issues with their vacation plans?

ANSWER: **Yes.** *Because the minimum age to rent a car in France is 21, Jenna and Marina will not be able to rent a car during their vacation. Furthermore, because the minimum age to drive in France is 18, and Marina is only 17, Marina would not be able to legally drive at all.*

NUDE BEACHES & CLOTHING-OPTIONAL RESORTS

IN THIS CHAPTER

- Overview
- Legality and Safety
- Tips for Nudist Tourists
- General Questions
- Law of the Land Hypothetical

NUDE BEACHES & CLOTHING-OPTIONAL RESORTS

Overview

Nudist culture is prominent in France, characterized by a long-standing tradition of naturism, with practices dating back to the 1920s. France is renowned for its liberal attitude toward nudity, offering a plethora of nude beaches and clothing-optional resorts that attract both locals and international visitors. The country boasts over 300 officially recognized naturist beaches, with popular destinations including *Cap d'Agde*, which is often considered the world's largest naturist resort, and *Plage de Tahiti* in Saint Tropez, famous for its vibrant social scene.

These locations provide a welcoming environment for individuals and families who wish to embrace a clothing-optional lifestyle in a natural setting, often accompanied by stunning coastal vistas and facilities that cater specifically to nudists. Additionally, numerous resorts across the country, such as *Euronat* and *CHM-Montalivet*, provide comprehensive amenities, including swimming pools, spas, and recreational activities while promoting a relaxed, naturist-friendly atmosphere. This unique cultural acceptance of nudism in France not only highlights the country's diverse recreational offerings but also fosters a sense of community and freedom among those who partake in this lifestyle.

Legality and Safety

Nudism in France is uniquely regulated, reflecting the country's liberal attitude toward nudity. Public nudity is permissible in designated areas such as naturist resorts, nude beaches, and private properties, and the laws support a culture where nudism can be practiced freely as long as it adheres to specific guidelines.[100] The French Penal Code does not criminalize nudism in these recognized environments; however, it explicitly prohibits any form of sexual exhibitionism in public spaces. This creates a legal framework that recognizes nudity as a legitimate lifestyle choice while ensuring a respectful atmosphere for all individuals.

Moreover, various local ordinances may impose additional regulations, such as restrictions on photography or the prevention of inappropriate behavior. The cultural acceptance of nudism varies by region, with certain areas, like Cap d'Agde, known as nudism-friendly zones, where such practices are more prevalent. This regional variance emphasizes the importance of respecting local customs and regulations, ensuring that nudism in France remains a socially acceptable and enjoyable experience for practitioners and visitors alike.

Nudist Etiquette

When visiting nudist beaches and resorts in France, it is essential to adhere to established etiquette to ensure a respectful and enjoyable experience for all participants. First and foremost, nudity should only be practiced in designated areas; stepping outside these boundaries while unclothed can lead to misunderstandings or legal repercussions. Visitors are advised to keep their distance from others to maintain personal space and privacy, allowing for a comfortable atmosphere. Taking photos is generally discouraged, as it can compromise the privacy of fellow nudists, and asking permission before capturing any images is a must. Moreover, while nudity is embraced, explicit sexual behavior is strictly prohibited in these environments, reinforcing the distinction between nudism and lewdness.

---

100 https://sandee.com/blog/nudism-laws-in-france

 **Tips for Nudist Tourists**

1. **Research the Destination:** Look for established nudist beaches or resorts with good reviews. Online forums and social media can provide insights from fellow travelers about safety and experiences.

2. **Local Regulations:** Familiarize yourself with the rules of the specific beach or resort. Some places may have designated areas for nudism, while others might be more lenient. Adhering to local customs helps ensure a positive experience.

3. **Travel in Groups:** If possible, visit with friends or fellow travelers. There's safety in numbers, and it can enhance the experience to share it with others.

4. **Stay Aware of Your Surroundings:** As with any beach or resort, it's wise to be aware of your environment. Keep personal belongings secure and be cautious of anyone acting suspiciously.

5. **Trust Your Instincts:** If a place feels uncomfortable or unwelcoming, it's okay to leave and seek another location.

6. **Respect Others' Privacy:** Nudist communities value consent and privacy. Always be respectful of others and avoid taking photos without permission.

 For more information, visit **naturisteparnature.fr** (in French) to easily locate naturist beaches and centers for your holiday. The *"Naturiste par Nature"* mobile app offers all the practical details you need for a successful naturist vacation, whether you're traveling with family, friends, alone, or as a couple. The app is available on both the App Store and Google Play.

General Questions

1. *Are there specific beaches in France that are well-known for nudism, and what should I know before visiting them?* Yes. France is home to several famous nudist beaches, including *Cap d'Agde* on the Mediterranean, *Plage de l'Espiguette* near Montpellier, and *Île du Levant* off the coast of Provence. Before visiting, ensure you're aware of the designated nudist areas, as nudity is not allowed everywhere. It's also important to follow local rules, be respectful of others, and check for any signs indicating where nudity is permitted. Some nudist beaches may require full nudity, while others are more relaxed about topless bathing.

2. *What should I wear when visiting a nude beach in France, and is it necessary to bring anything specific?* When visiting a nude beach in France, you're not required to wear anything, as nudity is the norm. However, if you're not comfortable being fully nude, toplessness is often accepted, and wearing a swimsuit is fine at many beaches. It's a good idea to bring a towel or beach mat to sit on, sunscreen to protect your skin, flip-flops for walking on hot sand, and a cover-up like a sarong for when you leave the beach or walk through public areas. Always check for signs to confirm where nudity is allowed and follow local rules.

3. *Is it safe to visit nude beaches in France?* Yes, it is generally safe to visit nude beaches in France. They are well-frequented by tourists and locals alike. However, as with any beach, it's important to be aware of your surroundings and follow any posted safety guidelines.

4. *Are there facilities like showers and restrooms at French nude beaches?* Yes. Many popular nude beaches in France have facilities such as showers and restrooms. However, the availability of these amenities can vary, so it's a good idea to check beforehand or be prepared for more basic conditions at less frequented beaches.

5. ***Can families visit nude beaches in France?* Yes**, families can visit nude beaches in France. These beaches are generally family-friendly, and nudism is often practiced as a natural and non-sexual lifestyle. However, it's always good to research and ensure the specific beach you plan to visit is suitable for children.

 ## Law of the Land Hypothetical

HYPOTHETICAL: *Linda and her teenage son, Jack, are from Canada and plan to visit a nude beach in Cap d'Agde. Linda is unsure if there are any age restrictions or if it is appropriate for Jack to visit the beach with her.*

ANSWER: *Linda and Jack can visit the nude beach in Cap d'Agde. French nude beaches are generally family-friendly and open to all ages, including teenagers. However, Linda should ensure that Jack feels comfortable and understands the etiquette and norms of nudism before visiting the beach.*

CHAPTER 20
UNUSUAL LAWS

UNUSUAL LAWS

Overview

Unusual laws can be fascinating glimpses into a culture's values and history. While most people are aware of common legal restrictions, it's often the strange and quirky laws that capture our attention. These regulations can range from the amusing to the absurd, reflecting the unique circumstances and traditions of a place. Whether they arise from historical events, societal norms, or simply peculiar local customs, unusual laws can provide insight into the quirks of human behavior and governance.

 ## France's Unusual Laws and Associated Penalties

France is known for its rich history, culture, and, of course, its unique and sometimes quirky laws. From bizarre regulations that date back to the Napoleonic era to those that seem designed to perplex outsiders, French bureaucracy can be as puzzling as it is intriguing. Here's a look at some of the more unusual laws that make France's legal landscape truly one-of-a-kind:

- **It is illegal to transport your snail by train without a ticket.** The fine for such offense is €7 (US$7.28)

- **It is illegal to be naked in your hotel room with the curtains open.** You could face a fine ranging from €15,000 to €30,000 (US$15,604.50 to $31,209) if you're caught exposed, even within the privacy of your hotel room or home.

- **Flying saucers are prohibited from flying over or landing in the southern French town of Châteauneuf-du-Pape,** which is internationally recognized for its unusual anti-UFO regulation.

- **It is technically illegal to kiss on the platform while a train is present.** This law was reportedly introduced to prevent couples from causing delays. The fine for violating this rule can be as high as €3,000 (US$3,120.90), though it is rarely enforced and is considered more of a "legal relic" from the past. Kissing must be done before the train arrives.

- **Unlimited self-service ketchup is banned in French school cafeterias.** In 2011, French authorities prohibited it, along with unlimited mayonnaise and vinaigrette, as part of a push to encourage healthier eating habits among children. However, ketchup is still allowed with specific meals, such as fries (*pommes frites*). The ban applies to all school and government cafeterias, except those serving fewer than 80 meals per day. Cafeterias are also required to keep records of what's served for health inspection purposes.

- **A mayoral decree in the tiny northern French village of Lhéraule demands a minimum level of politeness in the Town Hall.** The rules state that visitors can be asked to leave if they fail to use basic courtesies such as "hello," "thank you," and "goodbye." The decree was introduced after a rude taxpayer disrespected a civil servant in 2011.

- **French law requires that 40% of the music played on private radio stations must be of French origin.** Since 1996 the country's top media regulator, the *Conseil Supérieur de L'Audiovisuel*, has been charged with enforcing this rule. CSA also stipulates that half of the French music required by the quota be less than six months old.

- **It's illegal to drink alcohol at work, except for wine, beer, cider, pear cider, and a fermented honey drink called hydromel.** This means that any French company serving other types of alcohol at a *pot de départ* (farewell party) is technically breaking the law. However, the rules also stipulate that employers must send employees home if they are drunk, so moderation is key. Employers have a legal obligation to ensure the safety and health of their staff, and failure to comply could lead to civil or criminal penalties, with fines of up to €10,000 (US$10,403) per affected employee.

- **It is legal to marry a dead person.** This law stems back to when a dam burst in 1959 and killed 420 people in southern France. A pregnant woman who lost her fiancé was so upset that former President Charles de Gaulle penned a law allowing them to be married. However, the authorities require proof the couple planned to marry before one of them died.

- **It's legal for French parents to prevent their adult children from getting married.** A law dating back to the time of Napoléon Bonaparte allows parents to file an opposition to their child's marriage for any reason. This rule was invoked in 2010 when a Frenchman's family intervened to block his marriage to a Chinese woman, whom they believed was only seeking to secure her immigration status.

- **Bins and ashtrays are considered lethal weapons in Paris**, according to French penal code. Does that mean trash collectors' work is on par with bomb disposal units in terms of risk?

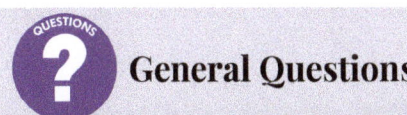

General Questions

1. *Is it illegal to wear camouflage clothing in France?* In France, wearing camouflage clothing as a civilian is not explicitly illegal, but it is generally considered inappropriate and could result in a fine if worn in a way that could be mistaken for a military uniform, particularly if it is causing public disturbance or confusion with military personnel. The exact penalty depends on the circumstances and local regulations.

2. *What happens if I fail to pay a fine in France?* If you do not pay within three months, the case will be transferred to the French Public Prosecutor, and you will have to pay the French Public Treasury (*Trésor Public*) an increased fine ranging from €180 (US$189.07) to €375 (US$393.82). It could also lead to difficulties when you try to re-enter France in the future due to an unpaid debt on your record; in some cases; your passport might even be temporarily held until the fine is settled.[101]

3. *Are there any laws about taking photos in France?* France's privacy laws are not new, and they are non-punitive in nature. They were primarily designed to protect individuals from paparazzi. It's generally acceptable to photograph people in public, as long as it doesn't cause harm, such as ridiculing them or exposing private information. These laws aren't what you would consider "strict" or "enforceable" in the traditional sense.[102]

 **Law of the Land True Story**

In 2008, a Frenchman learned the hard way that it's illegal to transport a snail on a train without a ticket. He and his pet snail were fined by the national rail operator SNCF when a conductor deemed the snail was fare-dodging. At the time, SNCF charged €7 for a pet ticket. After a media uproar, the passenger was refunded, but the rule remains in effect.[103]

101 https://www.sncf-voyageurs.com/en/customer-service/fines/

102 https://www.valeriejardinphotography.com/blog/2013/8/17/question-4-about-street-photography-privacy-laws#:~:text=The%20privacy%20laws%20in%20France,would%20consider%20'hard%20laws'.

103 https://www.thelocal.fr/20191204/france-facts-snails-need-a-ticket-to-travel-on-a-train

TRAVELING SAFELY

IN THIS CHAPTER

- Ladies Traveling Solo
- Traveling as a Family
- Advice for All Travelers
- Do's and Don'ts While in France
- General Questions
- Law of the Land True Story

CHAPTER 21

TRAVELING SAFELY

Ladies Traveling Solo[104]

France is largely considered a safe country for travelers, although it presents a nuanced safety landscape. While tourists may encounter issues such as petty crime, notably pickpocketing in crowded areas like Paris, violent crime rates remain relatively low compared to other global cities. The French government has implemented extensive security measures to combat terrorism and ensure public safety, especially surrounding major events such as the 2024 Olympics. Civil unrest and protests do occur, but these are typically peaceful and occur in designated areas. Overall, with standard precautions and vigilance, a majority of visitors experience a welcoming and secure environment during their travels in France.

Traveling alone as a woman in France is generally safe, with many female travelers reporting positive experiences across various regions. While popular cities like Paris and Lyon are largely welcoming, it's essential for solo female travelers to exercise caution and adhere to standard safety practices, particularly in crowded tourist areas. Some commonsense safety tips for a solo trip include:

- **Research your destination thoroughly:** Check current travel advisories and local news before visiting any area. Talk to the hotel or resort personnel or a trusted local what areas to avoid.

---

104 https://www.worldnomads.com/travel-safety/europe/france/womens-travel-in-france

- **Stick to well-populated areas:** Avoid venturing into isolated areas, especially at night.

- **Use licensed taxis and ride-sharing services:** Be cautious about using street taxis and always confirm the route with the driver. When traveling overnight, particularly on trains, opt for women-only or family compartments for added security.

- **Inform someone of your plans:** Let a trusted friend or family member know your itinerary and expected return times.

- **Be aware of your surroundings:** Stay vigilant and trust your instincts.

- **Dress modestly in certain areas:** Depending on the region, dressing conservatively can help you avoid unwanted attention.

- **Learn basic French phrases:** Knowing a few basic French phrases can be helpful for communication.

For more info on solo travel for women in France, visit **https://www.worldnomads.com/travel-safety/europe/france/womens-travel-in-france.**

Emergency Contacts for Women in Crisis

If you have been assaulted, you can call France's **national rape crisis hotline** at **0 800 059 595,** which is toll-free from any phone. This service is managed by *Viols Femmes Information*, a women's organization based in Paris (9 villa d'Este, 13e, Paris; Porte d'Ivry).

For immediate police assistance, dial **17.** Additionally, the **Association Maison des Femmes de Paris** (Phone: **01 43 43 41 13;** Address: 163 rue de Charenton, 12e, Paris; Reuilly Diderot) provides a safe space and resources for women in need.

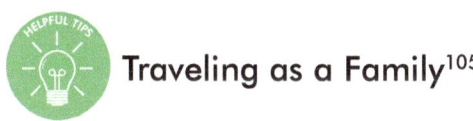

Traveling as a Family[105]

France is an ideal family vacation destination, offering a diverse range of experiences from sandy beaches to thrilling mountain adventures. Each region has its own unique charm, from the cultural richness of Paris to the outdoor wonders of the Alps. For a relaxing beach getaway, the South of France is perfect, with sun-drenched villages, picturesque markets, and family-friendly beaches. Whether you're seeking glamorous coastal towns or the more laid-back vibe of St. Tropez, there's something for everyone.

For adventurous families, skiing in the French Alps is a top choice, with world-class resorts like Chamonix, Val d'Isère, and Courchevel offering activities for all ages, from ski schools for young children to off-piste adventures for teens. In summer, the Alps also provide exciting activities like hiking and mountain biking, making it a year-round destination for family fun. Whether you're after history, relaxation, or adventure, France promises unforgettable memories for the whole family.

Safety and Health Precautions when Traveling with Children[106]

When traveling to France with children, it's important to take a few health and safety precautions to ensure a smooth trip.

General Safety Tips:

- Establish a meeting point in crowded areas in case of separation.
- Equip children with identification, such as a card with parents' contact information.
- Prefer buses over the metro for a less congested environment.

---

105 https://www.scottdunn.com/us/france/guides/family-holidays-france

106 https://www.smartraveller.gov.au/destinations/europe/france#:~:-text=Insect%2Dborne%20diseases,%2C%20loose%2C%20light%2Dcoloured%20clothing

- Maintain vigilance against petty crime and secure belongings in cross-body bags.

Health Considerations:

- Consult a healthcare provider for vaccinations before traveling.
- Pack a travel health kit with medications for common ailments.
- Familiarize with local healthcare services and emergency numbers (dial 15 for medical emergencies).
- Prioritize food safety by choosing cooked foods and encouraging hand washing.

Emergency Preparedness:

- Establish clear communication strategies with kids regarding emergencies.
- Carry a booklet with key phrases in French for effective communication.
- Pack an emergency bag with snacks, water, first-aid items, and identification documents for convenience.

Advice for All Travelers

Traveling in France offers a delightful experience filled with rich history and cultural vibrancy; however, travelers should be well-prepared to ensure a smooth visit. Safety is paramount, especially in tourist-heavy areas like Paris, where pickpocketing can occur. It is advisable to secure personal belongings and stay vigilant, while also familiarizing yourself with local emergency numbers for quick assistance (see *Important Emergency Numbers* at the end of the book).

Understanding cultural etiquette is equally important; greetings play a vital role, and visitors should greet locals with "Bonjour" when entering establishments. Dining in France is a leisurely affair, and patience is essential as meals are meant to be savored rather than rushed.

Additionally, navigating the extensive transportation options is key to a successful trip. The French train system is efficient, connecting cities quickly, while public transport in urban areas enhances accessibility. Travelers are encouraged to purchase tickets in advance and carry local transit maps for ease of navigation.

Embracing local customs enriches the travel experience; trying regional cuisine, exploring local markets, and practicing basic French phrases contribute to a deeper cultural immersion. By following these tips, visitors can enjoy all that France has to offer while creating lasting memories.

Do's and Don'ts While in France[107]

When visiting France, there are a few cultural norms and etiquette rules to keep in mind to ensure a respectful and enjoyable experience. Here are some important do's and don'ts to keep in mind:

Do's:

- **Learn Basic French Phrases:** While many people in France speak English, especially in tourist areas, making an effort to speak basic French (like "Bonjour" for hello and "Merci" for thank you) is appreciated.

- **Respect Meal Times:** Meals are an important part of French culture. Lunch is typically between 12:00 PM and 2:00 PM, and dinner starts around 7:30 PM or later. Try to avoid eating during off-hours.

- **Dress Smartly:** The French take pride in their fashion, and dressing neatly, especially when dining out or visiting cultural sites, is expected. Casual attire like shorts and flip-flops may not be appropriate in more formal settings.

---

107 https://www.budgetair.com.au/flights/france/dos-and-donts

- **Say "Bonjour" Upon Entering Shops:** It's polite to greet shop-keepers or anyone you interact with a "Bonjour" before asking questions or making a purchase.

- **Use Table Manners:** Keep your hands on the table (but not your elbows) and try not to start eating until everyone is served.

- **Tip Appropriately:** Tipping is appreciated but not mandatory in France, as service charges are typically included in restaurant bills. However, leaving small change (5-10%) for good service is common.

- **Be Punctual:** Arriving on time is valued, especially for appoint-ments, dinners, and business meetings. If you're going to be late, it's polite to inform your host.

Don'ts:

- **Don't Rush Your Meals:** In France, meals are social events. Avoid rushing through your food and enjoy the experience.

- **Don't Ask for Modifications to Dishes:** French chefs take pride in their cooking, so don't ask for substitutions or modifications to dishes unless there is a dietary restriction. Trust the chef's recommendations.

- **Don't Assume Everyone Speaks English:** While many people in tourist areas do speak English, don't assume everyone will. Always try to ask if someone speaks English before launching into it.

- **Don't Talk About Money or Politics Too Soon:** Avoid discuss-ing sensitive topics like money, politics, or religion, especially with strangers or acquaintances. Wait for the conversation to naturally move in those directions.

- **Don't Talk Loudly:** The French generally prefer a more subdued tone when in public, especially in restaurants, cafés, or museums. Avoid speaking loudly or drawing too much attention to yourself.

- **Don't Skip the Formalities:** When meeting someone, be sure to offer a handshake or a cheek kiss (typically two or three, depending on the region). Addressing people with "Monsieur" or "Madame" shows respect.

Interaction with Locals

Interacting with locals while traveling in France can significantly enrich the experience and offer unique insights into the country's vibrant culture. French people often appreciate when visitors make an effort to communicate in their native language, even if it means stumbling through basic phrases. Simple greetings such as *"Bonjour"* (hello) and *"Merci"* (thank you) go a long way in establishing rapport and showing respect for their culture. Engaging in small talk about local traditions, cuisine, or art can foster friendly connections; however, it is important to steer clear of personal questions regarding income or familial matters, as such topics may be deemed intrusive.

Additionally, visitors who show an appreciation for the country's renowned cuisine and cultural traditions are highly regarded. Exploring local markets, dining in small bistros, and trying regional specialties like *coq au vin* or *ratatouille* are ways to authentically engage with French culture. French people also value tourists who respect social norms and etiquette, such as greeting shopkeepers, waiting for the host to start meals, and practicing good table manners. Demonstrating patience in restaurants, where meals are savored rather than rushed, is also important. Tourists who engage in local life—whether by discussing regional politics, attending festivals, or exploring neighborhoods outside the typical tourist spots—further connect with the community and earn respect and good will of the locals.

General Questions

1. *What are some safety tips for using public transportation in France as a solo female traveler?* Using public transportation can be a safe and convenient way to get around France. However, it's important to keep your belongings close to you and be aware of your surroundings. It's also a good idea to avoid empty train cars and try to sit near other passengers. If you feel uncomfortable or unsafe, it's best to trust your instincts and get off at the next stop.

2. *Is it safe to walk alone at night in France?* While France is generally safe, it's still important to exercise caution when walking alone at night. Stick to well-lit areas and avoid empty streets or alleyways. It's also a good idea to let someone know where you're going and when you plan to return.

3. *What is the best time of year to visit France as a solo female traveler?* The best time to visit France depends on your preferences and itinerary. Summer is the peak tourist season, with warm weather and plenty of events and festivals. Spring and fall offer milder weather and fewer crowds, while winter can be cold but offers festive holiday markets and skiing opportunities.

Law of the Land True Story[108]

As you wander along the lively Boulevard Saint-Germain on the Left Bank, take a moment to appreciate three iconic landmarks of Parisian café culture near the Church of Saint-Germain-des-Prés: the Café des Deux Magots, the Café de Flore (right next door), and Brasserie Lipp (across the street). These historic cafés became the heart of Europe's

---

108 https://www.globusjourneys.in/vac-stories/cafe-society/

bohemian scene in the 1930s, attracting famous artists like Picasso, André Breton, Salvador Dalí, and Marcel Duchamp, along with a circle of writers, celebrities, and fashion icons. During the German occupation, intellectuals Jean-Paul Sartre and Simone de Beauvoir made the Flore their base, after being pushed out of their usual spots by Nazi officers. Living in a modest hotel at the time, they spent their days at the café, with Sartre later recounting their strict daily routine of writing, eating, socializing, and working late into the night. "The Flore was like home to us," Sartre wrote, even continuing to work through air-raid alarms. Today, these storied cafés remain perfect spots for people-watching and deep conversations, with the Deux Magots offering guests antique wooden desks rather than traditional tables. The small square in front of the Flore is now called Place Sartres-Beauvoir in honor of the iconic couple.

TOURIST TAXATION

TOURIST TAXATION

Tourist Taxes in France[109]

Tourists visiting France are required to pay a tourist tax, known as the *"taxe de séjour,"* which is structured to support local municipalities in managing and promoting tourism. This tax is generally applicable to travelers staying in commercial accommodation, such as hotels, bed and breakfasts, campsites, and furnished vacation rentals.[110] The amount of the tax can vary widely depending on the type of accommodation and its rating; for example, visitors may pay between €0.65 (US$0.68) per night for a basic campsite to as much as €14.95 (US$15.55) for luxury establishments.[111] This rate is typically charged per person, per night, making it essential for travelers to inquire about this fee when booking accommodations.

Additionally, some municipalities may charge additional fees or taxes, such as a "departmental additional tax," which is a percentage levied on the standard tourist tax to further support local tourism initiatives. This dual taxation system allows local authorities to enhance tourism

---

109 https://www.authentic-europe.com/travel-info/during-your-tour/tourist-taxes

110 https://www.connexionfrance.com/news/tourist-tax-who-pays-this-in-france-how-much-and-when/673673

111 https://parisjetaime.com/eng/article/tourist-tax-a616

infrastructure and maintain quality services, thereby improving the experience for visitors in France. Therefore, it is advisable for tourists to check the specific rates and regulations in the regions they intend to visit to ensure a clear understanding of the applicable fees during their stay.

In addition to the tourist tax, tourists in France may encounter other financial obligations, including a departure tax under specific circumstances. While France does not impose a general departure tax for all travelers, those who transfer their tax domicile outside of France may be subject to an exit tax if they meet certain criteria, such as having been a tax resident for at least six out of the previous ten years and holding unrealized capital gains exceeding €800,000 (US$832,240).[112] This tax, typically set at a flat rate of 30%, aims to levy taxes on the wealth accumulated within the country. However, for most casual tourists visiting France, there are no departure taxes applied upon leaving the country.

 **General Questions**[113]

1. ***Who collects the tourist tax? Do all guests have to pay the taxe de séjour?*** Accommodation providers are responsible for collecting taxes from guests. In some cases, guests may be required to pay the tax at the time of booking, while others may choose to collect it upon arrival. However, it is the property owner or manager's responsibility to remit the tax to the appropriate authorities, ensuring the correct amount is calculated and collected in accordance with local regulations. In most cases, all adult guests staying at the accommodation are required to pay the *taxe de séjour*. However, there are exceptions, including children under eighteen, individuals in emergency accommodation or temporary housing, and seasonal workers, who are typically exempt from the tax.

---

112 https://brighttax.com/blog/us-expat-taxes-in-france/

113 https://www.ovonetwork.com/blog/taxe-de-sejour-2/

2. ***How do guests know how much they have to pay?*** Guests can find out how much they need to pay for the tourist tax, primarily through the accommodation providers. Hotels, bed and breakfasts, and vacation rentals are required to inform guests about the tax amount at the time of booking and on the invoice upon check-in. Additionally, many property websites list the tax rates according to the type of accommodation, ensuring transparency. Travelers can also consult local tourist information offices or municipal websites to confirm the specific tax rates applicable in the area they are visiting, thereby ensuring they are adequately informed of any additional charges related to their stay.

3. ***What if the group size varies throughout the stay?*** To ensure the correct amount of tax is calculated and collected, booking details and contracts must match. Any necessary changes should be made before requesting the balance payment from guests. If guests are paying upon arrival, managers or agencies can make adjustments to the payment directly with guests at the resort.

 **Law of the Land Hypothetical**

HYPOTHETICAL: *Sarah, a British tourist, books a stay at a charming hotel in Paris for a week with her husband and two children. She completes her booking online, but when she arrives at the hotel, the manager informs her that she will need to pay the taxe de séjour (tourist tax) on top of her accommodation bill. Sarah is surprised, as she didn't see any mention of this extra charge when booking. The manager explains that the tax is calculated based on the number of adults in the room, and her children are exempt. Sarah wants to know if she's been charged the correct amount.*

ANSWER: *The manager is correct. In France, the taxe de séjour is a local tax levied on adults staying in tourist accommodations. The tax amount varies by location and type of accommodation. In Sarah's case,* *since only the two adults (Sarah and her husband) are considered for the tax, the children are exempt. As the hotel owner is responsible for calculating and collecting the correct amount, Sarah should check the tax rate for Paris (which may range from €1 to €5 per adult per night, depending on the hotel's star rating) to ensure the charge aligns with local regulations. If the charge seems incorrect, Sarah can request clarification from the hotel or consult the booking details to verify the rate.*

CHAPTER 23
LONG-TERM STAYS

CHAPTER 23

LONG-TERM STAYS

Overview[114]

People choose to stay long-term in France for a variety of compelling reasons, blending cultural, professional, educational, and lifestyle factors. Firstly, France boasts an exceptional quality of life characterized by a strong emphasis on work-life balance, comprehensive healthcare, and a rich cultural heritage. The country's renowned education system, which offers affordable tuition and excellent academic institutions, attracts many international students and families seeking quality education for their children. Moreover, France's diverse landscapes, from the picturesque countryside to vibrant urban centers, provide an appealing environment for those seeking both adventure and tranquility. Additionally, the strong expat communities found in cities like Paris and Lyon create a supportive network for newcomers, making it easier to navigate life in a new country.

Best Regions and Cities for Long-Term Living in France

When considering long-term living in France, several regions and cities stand out due to their quality of life, cultural richness, and affordability. Paris, the capital, offers a dynamic metropolitan lifestyle with world-class amenities, vibrant arts, and diverse job opportunities, although its

---

114 https://france-visas.gouv.fr/en/long-stay-visa

high cost of living can be a drawback. For a more affordable yet culturally rich experience, cities like Lyon and Bordeaux are excellent alternatives. Lyon is renowned for its gastronomy and historical significance, while Bordeaux is famous for its wine and picturesque architecture, both offering a strong sense of community and good public services.[115]

In the south, cities such as Montpellier and Nice appeal to those seeking a Mediterranean lifestyle with pleasant weather and access to beautiful coastlines. Montpellier is known for its youthful energy and academic environment, making it attractive for families and students. Meanwhile, Nice combines stunning coastal views with cultural events, catering to those looking for a laid-back lifestyle with ample leisure activities. Lastly, regions like Provence-Alpes-Côte d'Azur offer charming villages and a slower pace of life, ideal for expats seeking a tranquil but culturally vibrant environment.

Living Cost in France

Living costs in France present a nuanced landscape when compared to other countries, particularly the United States. On average, the cost of living in France is approximately 34% lower than in the United States, with the average monthly expenses for a single person in France estimated at around €1,800 (US$1,872.51), compared to US$3,308 for an individual in the U.S.[116] Although housing costs can be high in major French cities like Paris, everyday expenses such as groceries, utilities, and healthcare generally tend to be more affordable in France. For instance, healthcare premiums in France significantly undercut those in the U.S., where insurance costs can reach over US$8,400 annually, compared to just €979 (US$1,018.45) in France. Furthermore, dining out and shopping in France typically come at lower prices than in many American cities, providing a more comprehensive quality of life for less money.

---

115 https://internationalmoving.com/best-places-to-live-in-france-for-expats

116 https://www.expatistan.com/cost-of-living/country/united-states

Housing Options for Long-Term Stays

Visitors seeking long-term housing options in France have a variety of choices to suit different needs and budgets. One popular option is renting apartments or studios, which can range from small, furnished units in bustling urban centers to more spacious accommodations in suburban areas. Websites and platforms like Airbnb and MorningCroissant specialize in furnished rentals, offering the comforts of home for stays of a month or longer, often providing amenities such as kitchens and Wi-Fi.

Additionally, serviced apartments are an attractive choice for business travelers, as they offer hotel-like services in a residential setting, making them suitable for longer stays.[117] For those looking for affordable alternatives, shared housing arrangements, such as co-living spaces or house shares, allow individuals to live with others while keeping costs down. Local real estate websites and classified ads can also help visitors find long-term leases, providing access to a wider range of properties spread throughout various regions of France.

Transportation Options

Long-term visitors to France have a variety of transportation options that facilitate mobility throughout the country, ensuring they can easily explore both urban and rural areas. The French public transportation system is notably efficient and well-developed, with extensive rail networks operated by the *Société Nationale des Chemins de Fer Français* (SNCF) offering connections between major cities and smaller towns via high-speed trains like the TGV and regional services. In urban centers, the metro, trams, and bus networks provide convenient and affordable travel options. Cities like Paris, Lyon, and Marseille have comprehensive public transit systems that make getting around simple.

For those who prefer alternative modes of transport, bike-sharing programs, such as Vélib' in Paris, allow users to rent bicycles for short trips, promoting a healthy and eco-friendly way to navigate the city.

---

117 https://www.parisattitude.com/tenant/paris-furniture.aspx

Additionally, ride-sharing services, including Uber and local taxi services, are available in larger cities, providing greater flexibility for travelers. Car rentals can also be a viable option for visitors wanting to explore the picturesque French countryside, with many rental agencies offering a range of vehicles.

Healthcare Options for Long-Term Visitors

Long-term visitors in France have access to a range of healthcare options, primarily through the country's public healthcare system and private insurance plans. The French healthcare system, PUMA, provides comprehensive medical coverage to residents, including non-EU long-term visitors who have resided in France for at least three months. This public health insurance scheme typically covers around 70% of general practitioner visits and 80% of hospital expenses, although the proportion may vary based on individual circumstances and types of treatments.[118] To register for PUMA, visitors must apply through their local *Caisse Primaire d'Assurance Maladie* (CPAM) office, presenting required documentation such as proof of residence and identification.

In addition to the public healthcare system, many long-term visitors opt for private health insurance plans to complement their public coverage. Private insurance can help cover the remaining costs not included in the state coverage, such as excess charges, dental care, and specialist consultations, which might have lower reimbursement rates through the public system. Numerous international health insurance providers, such as Cigna and AXA, offer tailored plans for expatriates and long-term visitors, ensuring access to a wide network of healthcare services.[119]

Language Considerations

For foreign long-term visitors to France, navigating the language landscape is an essential consideration that can significantly enhance their

---

118 https://www.axaglobalhealthcare.com/en/international-health-insurance/france

119 https://www.cignaglobal.com/where-we-cover/france

experience in the country. While many urban residents, particularly in larger cities like Paris, have a conversational command of English, the dominant language is, unequivocally, French. Therefore, it is highly beneficial for visitors to learn basic French phrases to facilitate communication and show respect for the local culture (please refer to "Useful French Phrases" at the end of the book). Simple greetings, such as "Bonjour" (hello) and "Merci" (thank you), can go a long way in fostering positive interactions with locals, as the French tend to appreciate efforts to engage in their native language.

Moreover, understanding the nuances of the French language, including its formal and informal forms of address, is critical in social settings. The distinction between "vous" (formal) and "tu" (informal) reflects social hierarchies and helps establish the appropriate level of politeness in conversations. Furthermore, for those staying long-term, enrolling in a French language course can not only improve conversational skills but also deepen cultural understanding, opening new avenues for making connections and fully immersing in the French way of life. While prior knowledge of French is not strictly necessary for survival, making an effort to learn the language will enrich the experience and enable more meaningful engagement with the local community.

Long-Term Visas

Before applying for a long-term visa, it's essential to check whether your nationality or specific circumstances exempt you from visa requirements. Long-term visas for France are available for the following purposes:

- Tourism or personal reasons
- Professional activities
- Education
- Family reunification

For any of these, you must submit supporting documents related to your specific situation and follow the relevant procedures.

Application Process:

1. **Apply through France-Visas:** Start by completing the online application via the official France-Visas website. The Visa Assistant will help determine if you need a visa and guide you through the process. You can track your application status online.

2. **Submission:** The application must be submitted to the French embassy, consulate, or external service provider (e.g., VFS Global or TLS) in your country of residence, no earlier than three months before your planned arrival date.

Required Documents:

Documents needed will vary depending on the visa category (tourism, work, study, etc.) and the type of residence permit you plan to apply for when your visa expires. The Visa Assistant on the France-Visas website provides a detailed list of required documents based on the reason for your stay.

Costs:

The visa application fee is €99 (US$102.99), payable when submitting your application. This fee applies to all visa categories and is non-refundable, even if the application is rejected.

 For further details, you can check the specific requirements and fees on the official France-Visas website at **https://france-visas.gouv.fr/en/**

Residency Requirements for Foreigners

To become a resident in France, foreigners typically need to meet several requirements, starting with applying for a long-stay visa. Once granted, you can apply for a residence permit (Carte de Séjour) to live in France for an extended period. To qualify for a permanent residence permit (Carte de Résident), you usually need to have lived in France for five years with a valid residence permit, or three years if you are married to a French national.

Key requirements include:

1. **Financial Stability:** You must prove you can financially support yourself, often by showing employment contracts or bank statements. The income must typically exceed the French minimum wage.

2. **Integration and Language:** Demonstrating integration into French society is important, which may involve learning French and understanding French culture. You may need to sign a Republican Integration Contract (*Contrat d'Intégration Républicaine*).

3. **Health Insurance:** You must have valid health insurance, either through private insurance or the French social security system.

4. **Other Documentation:** You may need to provide a birth certificate, undergo medical exams, and prove you are not a threat to public order or national security.

These requirements ensure that applicants are self-sufficient, integrated, and able to contribute to French society.

General Questions

1. *How do I prove my accommodation in France?* If you're renting, provide a copy of the lease. If you're staying with someone, a certificate from your host and a copy of their ID are needed.

2. *What happens if I overstay my visa?* Overstaying your visa can lead to penalties, including refusal of entry or deportation. Any future visa applications might also be refused.

3. *What income requirements are there for a long-stay visa?* You'll typically need to demonstrate sufficient income, often exceeding the French minimum wage, around €1,766.92 (US$1,838.13) per month gross.

4. *If I want to stay in France long-term and work, should I apply for a work permit before arriving in France?* **Yes**, you must apply for a work visa before arriving in France if you want to stay long-term and work. This requires having a job offer from a French employer, after which you can apply for a long-stay work visa at the French embassy or consulate in your home country. Once in France, you may need to register for a *Carte de Séjour* (residence permit) to continue working legally.

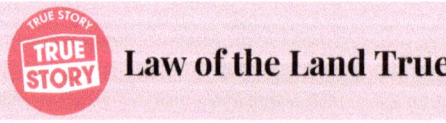

Law of the Land True Story[120]

Amadou moved to France from Mali in 2001 on a work visa but overstayed, which is a common path to becoming an undocumented migrant in Europe. He has worked continuously in the hospitality and retirement sectors for 19 years without taking holidays or sick days.

---

120 https://www.france24.com/en/france/20231222-france-s-undocument-ed-migrants-face-uncertain-future-under-new-immigration-bill

Despite applying for working papers twice—once in 2012 and again in 2018—he was denied both times, with the 2018 application rejected due to his lack of dependents. Since then, he has been unable to secure another opportunity to apply, despite support from his employer.

Takeaways

- **Visa Options and Application Process:** To stay long-term in France, foreign nationals must apply for a long-stay visa based on the purpose of their stay (tourism, work, education, or family re-unification). The application must be made through the official France-Visas website, and documents will vary depending on the type of visa.

- **Best Regions and Cities for Expats:** France offers a wide range of appealing cities for long-term living. Paris, Lyon, Bordeaux, and Montpellier stand out for their quality of life, cultural richness, and expat communities. Southern cities like Nice and Montpellier are also attractive for those seeking a Mediterranean lifestyle.

- **Living Costs and Affordability:** France's cost of living is lower than in the U.S., with lower costs for healthcare, groceries, and dining out. Housing costs can be high in major cities, but alternatives like co-living spaces or furnished rentals are available for those seeking more affordable options.

- **Healthcare and Insurance:** Long-term visitors have access to France's public healthcare system (PUMA), which covers most medical expenses. Private health insurance is also available to complement public coverage and provide additional services.

- **Residency and Work Requirements:** To qualify for permanent residency in France, foreigners generally need to have lived in France for five years with a valid residence permit (or three years for spouses of French nationals). Financial stability, health insurance, and cultural integration (including learning French) are key requirements.

- **Housing and Transportation:** Long-term visitors can rent apartments or use serviced apartments for a more hotel-like experience. The French public transportation system, including metro, buses, and trains, offers easy mobility, while bike-sharing programs and ride-sharing services are also available for flexible transport options.

CIVIL LITIGATION

CIVIL LITIGATION

Overview

Civil litigation provides a mechanism for resolving disputes, ensuring that travelers have a way to seek justice if legal issues arise while visiting another country. It helps them understand their rights and obligations under local laws, which may differ from those in their home country. The civil litigation system offers a formal process for addressing conflicts, such as contract disputes or personal injury claims, and can deter unfair practices by encouraging businesses to comply with legal standards. It also allows individuals to seek financial recourse for damages or losses and helps protect them from potential exploitation by local entities. Overall, understanding civil litigation enhances a visitor's experience and safety while traveling.

 ## Personal Injury and Compensation Law[121]

Personal injury law in France encompasses various regulations aimed at offering proper treatment and compensation to individuals harmed through the negligence of others. The legal framework plays a crucial role for victims of accidents, medical negligence, and workplace injuries,

---

121 https://www.holidaycare.org.uk/holiday-accident-claims/
france-holiday-accident-claims#1

all of which necessitate a thorough understanding of the compensation claim process.

Legal claims under French law are grounded in civil liability principles. The injured party must demonstrate that the defendant was at fault, that damage occurred, and that there is a direct link between the two. The French system is predominantly fault-based, allowing full reparation for the damages suffered, differing from other jurisdictions where limitations may be placed on claims.

Common personal injury claims in France include those from road traffic accidents, medical negligence, and public place accidents. For example, auto accident claims benefit from legislation providing automatic compensation for injuries caused by motor vehicles, barring "inexcusable fault" by the victim. Additionally, the *"Nomenclature Dinthillac,"* a specific classification system used in French law to categorize certain offenses, assists courts and insurers in categorizing and calculating damages.

Compensation policies seek to offer full reparation for both physical and psychological damages incurred by the victim. This encompasses medical costs, pain and suffering, and loss of earnings. Victims experiencing deterioration post-settlement can claim further compensation, underscoring the complexities of long-term rehabilitation.

Insurance is vital in the French personal injury claim process, facilitating smoother compensation for victims through liability insurers. The ability to claim directly against insurers simplifies the process. However, disputes may arise due to coverage complexities.

 # How to File a Civil Claim[122]

Filing a civil claim in France entails a systematic process rooted in French civil procedure. Initially, the claimant must serve a writ of summons, known as an "assignation," which outlines the grounds for the claim and details the specific relief sought. This document must be delivered to the defendant, usually by a bailiff, at least 15 days before the scheduled court date. The writ should include all necessary supporting documentation, including evidence that demonstrates the validity of the claim. If mediation or conciliation is required by law due to the nature of the dispute, the claimant must detail the steps undertaken before initiating court proceedings. This preliminary approach highlights the French legal system's emphasis on resolving disputes amicably whenever possible, a principle that can greatly influence the handling of civil claims.

Once the writ has been served, the court conducts a procedural phase where both parties exchange their arguments and evidence. The initial phase culminates in a trial hearing where oral arguments are presented, but it is important to note that decisions are not typically rendered on the same day; rather, they may take weeks or even months before a written judgment is released. The claimant may need to engage legal counsel throughout this process, as representation is often mandatory, especially in higher courts. Furthermore, claimants should be aware of the various costs associated with legal proceedings, including court fees and potential expenses for expert testimonies, which may influence their decision to proceed or seek resolution through other means like alternative dispute resolution. A thorough understanding of these procedural requirements is essential for effectively navigating the civil claim process in France.

---

122 https://iclg.com/practice-areas/
litigation-and-dispute-resolution-laws-and-regulations/france

How to File a Criminal Claim

Filing a criminal claim in France typically begins with reporting an offense to the police or *gendarmerie*, where the victim or a witness can either submit a formal complaint, known as a *"plainte,"* or provide a denunciation. It is essential to gather relevant documentation, such as identification and any evidence related to the offense, before making the initial report. The police are obligated to record the complaint and initiate an official investigation into the allegations, which includes gathering information, interviewing witnesses, and collecting evidence. If the complaint is considered serious, it may be passed to the public prosecutor's office (*Ministère public*), which has the authority to determine whether to press charges. Victims may also opt to file a civil action alongside the criminal claim if they seek damages for harm suffered during the crime.

Once the police initiate their investigation, they compile a dossier that includes all relevant information and evidence collected during the process. The public prosecutor then reviews the dossier to determine if there is sufficient evidence to proceed with prosecution. If the prosecutor decides to move forward, the case will be brought before a criminal court. It is important for the victim to stay informed throughout the process and consider seeking legal representation, which can be beneficial in navigating the complexities of the French criminal justice system. Additionally, French law allows for victims to directly participate in the proceedings as a civil party, which provides them with additional rights, such as the ability to seek compensation for damages during the criminal trial. Understanding these steps ensures that victims can effectively engage with the legal system when seeking justice for criminal offenses.

 ## Service of Documents

The service of documents in France is governed primarily by the provisions set forth in the Hague Service Convention, which mandates specific procedures for serving legal documents across international borders. In France, there are generally two recognized methods for serving documents: through the French Central Authority or via a *"huissier de justice,"* the court-appointed bailiff responsible for executing service in civil matters.[123] The process typically begins with the plaintiff submitting the necessary documents, including a request for service and any pertinent translations, to the selected authority. It is critical to note that documents must be translated into French to comply with the French regulations, as failing to provide proper translations may lead to the rejection of the service request by the Central Authority.

Once the documents are served, the bailiff or Central Authority is responsible for providing proof of service, which is crucial for the integrity of the legal process. In civil proceedings, service can sometimes be delayed, taking several weeks or even months, depending on the method chosen and the complexity of the case. Furthermore, it is important for legal practitioners to be aware that direct access to serve documents by a bailiff can expedite the process, especially in urgent situations; however, navigating this method may require proficiency in French or assistance from a local legal professional.[124] Compliance with the established protocols for service is essential, as improper service can lead to complications, including the potential dismissal of cases on procedural grounds.

Statute of Limitations[125]

The statute of limitations in France plays a crucial role in civil law by setting time limits for individuals to initiate legal actions, thereby promoting legal certainty and enabling the resolution of disputes within a reasonable time frame. In general, the standard limitation period for civil and commercial claims is five years, commencing from the date the claimant became aware or should have become aware of the facts giving rise to the cause of action. Certain types of claims, however, are subject

---

123 https://www.dgrlegal.com/international-service-of-process-in-france/

124 https://www.legallanguage.com/international-litigation/
service-of-process/countries/france

125 https://www.google.com/search?sca_esv=31fe99a6d4a2597d&q=Stat-
ute+of+limitations+France+Civil&sa=X&ved=2ahUKEwjM5YSt-
nbSKAxXFmrAFHVAzHfsQ1QJ6BAhKEAE&biw=1280&bih=863&dpr=1

to different limitation periods. For instance, personal injury actions are subject to a ten-year limitation period, while actions related to real estate issues extend up to thirty years, reflecting the legal system's recognition of the complexities involved in various types of claims. Such provisions underscore the importance of being vigilant about time frames, as failure to act within the stipulated periods can result in the loss of the right to pursue legal remedies.

Moreover, French law provides mechanisms for the interruption or suspension of limitation periods, which can significantly affect the ability to initiate proceedings. For example, if a claimant initiates litigation or sends a formal notification of their intent to pursue a claim, the limitation period may be interrupted, resetting the countdown. Additionally, specific circumstances, such as the legal incapacity of a party or ongoing negotiations between parties, may result in the suspension of the limitations period. It is essential for individuals seeking to protect their rights under French law to be aware of these provisions, as the statute of limitations not only influences access to justice but also encourages parties to engage in timely conflict resolution.

Getting Married in France[126]

You can get married in France while on your dream vacation, however, it comes with specific legal requirements that must be met to ensure the marriage is recognized. Foreign nationals can tie the knot in France, but at least one of the parties must meet residency conditions; specifically, one of them must have lived in the town where the marriage will take place for at least 30 consecutive days prior to the wedding. This residency requirement ensures a genuine connection to the locale, which French authorities prioritize. Notably, if both parties are foreigners and do not reside in France, they can still marry, but only at their respective embassies or consulates rather than through local municipal authorities.[127]

In addition to the residency principle, visitors must provide certain documentation to get married in France. Essential documents include valid passports or identification cards, birth certificates (which should not be older than six months), and a certificate of celibacy, confirming that the parties involved are not currently married. These documents must either be in French or translated by a certified translator. Once the necessary paperwork is in order, couples must file their marriage application at the local town hall (*mairie*), where they will also publish the marriage banns.

---

126 https://www.chateau-boisrigaud.fr/en/blog/
how-to-get-married-in-france/

127 https://www.service-public.fr/particuliers/vosdroits/F930?lang=en

In general, civil wedding ceremonies conducted at the local town hall (*mairie*) are relatively affordable, with standard fees ranging from €100 (US$104.03) to €700 (US$728.21).[128] These fees cover the administrative aspects of the marriage, such as the preparation of necessary documents and the official ceremonies conducted by a local civil authority, which are essential components of the legal marriage process in France.[129] However, couples should keep in mind that these are only the basic fees for the civil ceremony. Additional costs may arise if couples opt for supplementary services such as venue rentals, photography, catering, or floral arrangements for celebrations that extend beyond the civil ceremony.

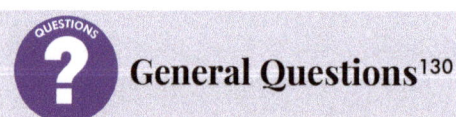

General Questions[130]

1. ***How long will the claim take?*** The timing of settling a claim depends on the cooperation of the defendant or their insurers, as well as how long it takes for you to recover. It's important not to settle too early, as claims are settled on a "once and for all" basis, meaning you cannot seek further compensation if recovery takes longer than expected. However, we ensure there are no unnecessary delays—if the opposing party is stalling, we will initiate civil court proceedings to apply pressure.

---

128 https://www.fevrierphoto.com/post/civil-wedding-ceremony-in-france

129 https://www.expatica.com/fr/living/love/getting-married-in-france-101112/

130 https://alysonfrance.co.uk/frequently-asked-questions/

2. ***Why do I need to see another medical professional?*** I'm already receiving care from my doctor or a hospital. While your doctor or the hospital focuses on your recovery, for your claim, a detailed medical report outlining your injuries and prognosis is required to assess your compensation. Typically, your own doctor is not considered "independent" in the context of a claim.

3. ***Do I need to use a French lawyer for my claim?*** It depends on the nature of your case. For most claims in France, particularly those involving the courts, it is recommended or even required to have a French lawyer (*avocat*). However, for some types of claims, such as small claims or administrative matters, you may not need a lawyer. It's always a good idea to consult with a lawyer familiar with French legal procedures to ensure your claim is handled correctly.

Law of the Land Hypothetical

HYPOTHETICAL: *A tourist from the United States was visiting Paris and enjoying a walk along the Seine River. As she was crossing a busy street near the Notre-Dame Cathedral, she was struck by a scooter that was speeding on a sidewalk, a common issue in some areas of the city due to the increasing number of rental electric scooters.*

The tourist, who was not familiar with the French road rules or how scooters operated in the area, was knocked over, resulting in a broken ankle and a severely sprained wrist. The scooter rider, a local Parisian, was initially apologetic, but the incident became more complicated when the tourist needed medical attention. What steps does the injured tourist need to take to assert her personal injury claim?

ANSWER: *First, seek immediate medical attention. In this case, the tourist was taken to a nearby hospital where her ankle was placed in a cast, and she was advised to rest while healing. It's essential to keep* records of any medical treatments received, as these will be necessary for insurance and legal purposes.

Next, contact your travel insurance company to report the injury. The insurance may cover some medical costs. Additionally, you should consider the possibility of taking legal action against the responsible party, such as the scooter rider in this case, especially if their negligence contributed to the accident. The rider's reckless use of the sidewalk could be grounds for a claim.

Under French law, tourists are entitled to seek compensation for injuries caused by negligence, including accidents involving electric scooters. The scooter company could also be investigated if it failed to ensure that users followed safety guidelines.

Finally, consult with a local lawyer who specializes in personal injury claims. The lawyer will guide you through the process of seeking compensation for medical bills and any disruption to your vacation. In this case, the scooter rider was found responsible for not following traffic rules, and compensation was awarded through the scooter company's liability insurance.

CHAPTER 25

OTHER THINGS TO KNOW

IN THIS CHAPTER

- Tourists and Street Hustling
- Safety Concerns and Practical Tips
- In the Event of Death
- Experiencing Financial Hardship
- General Questions
- Law of the Land Hypothetical

CHAPTER 25
OTHER THINGS TO KNOW

 **Tourists and Street Hustling**[131]

Street hustling in France is a common issue, particularly in tourist-heavy areas like Paris, Nice, and Marseille. In these popular destinations, visitors are often targeted by various scams and deceptive practices. The Eiffel Tower, Sacré-Cœur, and the Champs-Élysées in Paris, for example, are notorious for hustlers who prey on unsuspecting tourists. One of the most common scams is the "ring hustle," where scammers pretend to find a gold ring on the ground and attempt to sell it to tourists at an inflated price. Another frequent trick is the "friendship bracelet scam," where a person offers to tie a free bracelet on a tourist's wrist and then demands payment once it's in place. Some street hustlers also pose as representatives of fake charities, asking for donations under false pretenses. Additionally, selling counterfeit or low-quality artwork and souvenirs as genuine is widespread, with the "signature" scam involving an artist convincing tourists to purchase overpriced pieces from a supposed famous local artist. Lastly, the "change" scam involves a vendor claiming they don't have enough change, requesting a large bill, and then giving back less change than owed.

---

131 https://tinyurl.com/5cf9t7pj

Pickpocketing is also a major concern, especially in crowded spaces like subway stations and famous landmarks. Tourists, distracted by the sights and sounds, are often unaware of the pickpockets working the area.

In addition to these scams, street vendors in France frequently sell cheap souvenirs, such as replica Eiffel Towers, keychains, and trinkets. While these items are often sold at much lower prices than in legitimate shops, the quality is typically subpar, as many are mass-produced and lack authenticity. Food vendors, offering treats like crepes, ice cream, and drinks, are another feature of the street hustling scene. While tempting, tourists should be cautious, as hygiene standards and food quality may not always meet French regulations.

Street hustlers in France often provide services such as guided tours or street performances, including musicians and artists. These services can be enjoyable but are frequently unlicensed or unauthentic, raising concerns about their legitimacy.

The hustle is particularly prevalent in busy tourist zones in cities like Paris, Nice, and Marseille. In Paris, Montmartre is another hot spot, with its lively atmosphere often attracting street vendors and performers, many of whom engage in deceptive practices like the friendship bracelet scam. Similarly, in Nice, the Promenade des Anglais and the Old Town attract street hustlers, capitalizing on the influx of tourists seeking to enjoy the Mediterranean ambiance. In Marseille, the Old Port area sees a variety of scams, particularly around food vendors and street performers. These bustling areas provide fertile ground for hustlers, who take advantage of the high foot traffic and the often unsuspecting nature of tourists.

Street hustling in France presents a challenge for visitors, who may unknowingly fall victim to scams, low-quality goods, or unlicensed services. Awareness and vigilance are key to avoiding such deceptive practices and ensuring a safer and more enjoyable experience.

Safety Concerns and Practical Tips

Street hustling in France raises several safety concerns for tourists, primarily pertaining to petty crime, fraud, and even potential harassment. With crowded tourist areas attracting numerous visiting individuals, street hustlers often employ deceptive tactics that can lead to theft. Common scams, such as pickpocketing or distraction techniques, leverage the chaos of busy streets, where tourists may be more focused on their surroundings or taking photographs than on safeguarding their belongings.

Tourists, often unfamiliar with local customs and scams, can find themselves vulnerable to losing their wallets, phones, or personal items without even realizing it until it's too late. Additionally, the presence of aggressive vendors selling counterfeit goods may lead to uncomfortable situations, where refusal to buy can provoke hostility or harassment, detracting from the enjoyment of the travel experience.

Moreover, the issue of public safety extends beyond simple theft. The interactions with street hustlers can also create an intimidating environment for tourists. In certain cases, individuals posing as helpful locals may have ulterior motives, contributing to feelings of discomfort or fear among visitors. There have also been reports of more organized group crimes, where pickpockets operate in tandem with street performers or beggars to create distractions while they steal from heedless tourists. This kind of coordinated behavior can lead to a heightened sense of anxiety for travelers, particularly for those traveling alone or unfamiliar with the locale. Ultimately, these safety concerns underscore the importance of awareness, vigilance, and caution when navigating busy tourist areas in France, as tourists seek to enjoy their experiences while remaining protected from potential risks associated with street hustling.

To effectively navigate street hustling in France, tourists should adopt a series of practical strategies aimed at enhancing their safety and overall experience. Firstly, it is wise to remain vigilant and aware of your surroundings, particularly in crowded areas where hustlers are likely to operate. Keep your belongings secure in anti-theft bags and avoid displaying valuables such as expensive cameras, smartphones, and jewelry, as these can attract unwanted attention. Additionally, it is advisable to resist engaging with street vendors and performers who approach you quickly, particularly those offering unsolicited services or gifts, such as friendship bracelets. Politely declining any offers and continuing on your way can prevent potential entanglement in scams. Utilizing reputable local guides or organized tours can also ensure a safer exploration of popular attractions, while educating yourself about common scams can prepare you to recognize suspicious behavior. Lastly, trust your instincts—if something feels off, it may be best to remove yourself from the situation and seek help from local authorities or other tourists. By employing these tips, visitors can enjoy their time in France without falling victim to street hustling tactics.

 ## In the Event of Death

If you are visiting France and experience a death of someone you know, the first crucial step is to contact the nearest U.S. embassy or consulate to report the death and receive assistance with navigating the local procedures for handling the deceased, including coordinating with a local funeral home and obtaining necessary documentation to transport the remains back to the U.S. if needed; they will also try to locate and inform the next of kin.

The process may vary depending on the specific circumstances of the death, but in general, French authorities work closely with the deceased's family, the embassy, and local funeral services to handle the situation in a respectful and efficient manner. Key actions to take:

- **Notification of Authorities:** Inform the local authorities (police or gendarmerie) about the death. In cases of an unexpected death, the police will investigate the cause, especially if there are concerns about foul play, an accident, or a medical issue.

- **Death Certificate:** A local doctor or coroner must issue a death certificate. If the cause of death is clear (e.g., natural causes), a doctor who examines the body can provide it. If the cause is unclear or suspicious, an autopsy may be required.

- **Notification to the Embassy or Consulate:** Notify the tourist's home country embassy or consulate. They can assist with legal matters, provide support to the family, and help with repatriation if needed.

- **Repatriation of the Body:** The family may choose to have the body repatriated to their home country. This is arranged through a funeral home in France, which will manage the transportation and legal documentation for repatriation. Insurance may help cover these costs, if available. Alternatively, the family may choose burial in France, and the funeral service will manage the logistics.

- **Funeral and Burial:** If the family opts for burial or cremation in France, funeral services will help arrange these procedures, and burial may take place in a local cemetery.

- **Investigation and Legal Matters:** If the death is suspicious or involves a criminal investigation, the police will conduct an inquiry, including an autopsy and interviews. The investigation will determine if foul play or an accident was involved.

- **Handling of Personal Effects:** Authorities will secure the deceased's belongings. The embassy or consulate can assist in returning personal effects (e.g., passport, luggage) to the family, and inform them about how these items are handled.

- **Financial and Insurance Considerations:** If the deceased had travel insurance, it may cover costs for repatriation, funeral services, and medical expenses. The family should contact the insurance provider. If no insurance is available, the family will need to cover these expenses themselves.

 ## Experiencing Financial Hardship

If you are a U.S. citizen facing financial hardship while abroad, the first step is to contact the nearest U.S. embassy or consulate or reach the U.S. Department of State's Office of Overseas Citizens Services at +1 202-501-4444. They can help you by arranging funds from family, your bank, your employer, or, in some cases, wiring funds directly to you. You may also be eligible for a repatriation loan to cover return travel costs, including transportation, food, lodging, and medical expenses. Additionally, commercial money transfer services like Western Union or MoneyGram can help you receive funds quickly. If necessary, selling valuables could provide you with immediate cash.

To make your remaining funds stretch, consider affordable accommodation options like hostels, buying meals at local markets, and using public transportation. If permitted by your visa, you might explore short-term work opportunities, such as teaching English or freelancing. Contact your bank or credit card company for emergency funds or higher ATM withdrawal limits. Always be cautious of scams and trust your instincts. Once stabilized, create a daily budget and document all transactions and communications for clarity.

In France, tourists experiencing financial hardship have several support options:

- **Tourism Information Centers** (*Office de Tourisme*) offer details on affordable accommodation, meals, and local charities.

- **Emergency Assistance** from organizations like the **French Red Cross** or **local Social Services** (**CCAS**) can help with housing, food, or transportation.

- **NGOs and Charities** such as **Secours Catholique** and **Restos du Cœur** provide food, shelter, and other aid.

- **Crowdfunding** through platforms like **GoFundMe** or **Leetchi** allows you to seek financial assistance from friends, family, or strangers.

- **Emergency Loans** may be available from some French banks, with requirements like proof of ID and a return ticket.
- **Transportation Aid:** Services like **SNCF** and local transport may offer discounted or free rides in emergencies.
- **Local Community Groups** and online forums (such as expat groups or social media) may offer advice or direct assistance.

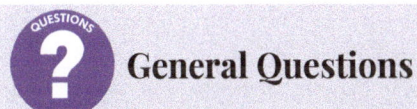

General Questions

1. *Is street hustling more common in certain seasons in France?*
   Yes. Street hustling tends to increase during the tourist season (spring and summer), when there are more visitors in the cities. Additionally, the holiday seasons, especially around Christmas, see an uptick in scams due to the increased crowds and tourists shopping for gifts.

2. *What should you do if you fall victim to a hustle in France?*
   If you are pickpocketed or scammed, it's important to stay calm and avoid reacting emotionally. Try to remember details about the person responsible. Report the theft to local authorities, as they may recover stolen items or help identify the thief. If your wallet is stolen, immediately contact your bank to cancel any lost or stolen credit cards. Additionally, if your passport is stolen, reach out to your embassy or consulate for assistance.

 **Law of the Land Hypothetical**

HYPOTHETICAL: *While vacationing in Paris, you're leisurely strolling through the lively streets of Montmartre, taking in the charming cobblestone paths and the breathtaking view of the Sacré-Cœur Basilica. A friendly man approaches, flashing a quick smile and offering a deck of cards. He invites you to play a simple game: find the queen among three cards. The game seems easy enough. He shuffles the cards expertly, and you correctly guess in his demo rounds. Feeling confident, you place a small bet. He shuffles again, and you're certain you know where the queen is. You point confidently, only to discover the queen isn't there. What just happened?*

ANSWER: You've fallen for the classic "three-card monte" or "bonneteau," a well-known street scam. The hustler uses sleight of hand to ensure you never win. To make the scam more convincing, his accomplices, posing as innocent bystanders, cheer you on or even pretend to win, building your confidence and encouraging you to play again. There are a few important lessons to remember from this scenario: trust your instincts—if something feels too good to be true, it likely is; avoid street games, especially those involving money, as they are almost always rigged; stay aware of your surroundings, as scammers often work in groups to distract and manipulate; and always guard your valuables, as another accomplice might be picking your pocket while you're distracted.

QUICK REFERENCE GUIDE

QUICK REFERENCE GUIDE

Crime in France

Are there particular areas I should avoid as a tourist?

Yes. While France is generally safe for tourists, there are certain areas where you should exercise caution, especially in Paris (northern suburbs, Gare du Nord, and Montmartre at night), Marseille (north neighborhoods and Gare Saint-Charles), and Nice (late-night Promenade des Anglais). Avoid high-crime outskirts in cities like Lyon and Toulouse. Always stay aware of scams, particularly in crowded spots, and avoid isolated areas after dark. Stick to well-lit, busy areas, and be vigilant with your belongings. *For more details, see Chapter 3.*

Drug Offenses

Is the possession of marijuana legal?

No. Possession of marijuana for personal use is illegal in France, although recent reforms have introduced fines for minor possession offenses. Possession of up to 100 grams of cannabis can lead to an on-the-spot fine of €200 (US$208.06), which can be reduced to €150 (US$156.04) if paid within 15 days, or increased to €450 (US$468.13) if paid after 45 days.

Is the possession of cocaine legal?

> **No.** The possession of cocaine is **illegal** in France. Penalties can include fines, imprisonment for up to 10 years, or both, depending on the amount and whether trafficking is suspected. *For more details, see Chapter 4.*

Alcohol-Related Offenses

What is the legal drinking age?

> The legal drinking age in France is **18** years old. This applies to both the purchase and consumption of alcoholic beverages, including beer, wine, and spirits.

What is the legal blood alcohol limit?

> The legal blood alcohol limit for drivers is **0.05%** (50 mg of alcohol per 100 ml of blood). However, for novice drivers (those with less than three years of driving experience), the limit is stricter at **0.02%** (20 mg per 100 ml). If you're caught driving under the influence, you may face fines, license suspension, or even imprisonment, depending on the severity of the offense. *For more details, see Chapter 5.*

Firearm & Ammunition Offenses

Can I possess a gun?

> Generally, private individuals cannot possess firearms without a specific license. Guns are classified into different categories based on their potential danger, and possession is only allowed under strict conditions, such as for hunting, sport shooting, or collecting. You must undergo background checks, training, and obtain authorization from local authorities. Automatic weapons and most semi-automatic firearms are prohibited for civilian use.

Can I possess ammunition?

> The possession of ammunition is also regulated and typically requires a license. You cannot possess ammunition without a corresponding firearm license, and certain types of ammunition are

restricted or prohibited. For example, ammunition for firearms classified as restricted or prohibited is illegal to possess without specific authorization. *For more details, see Chapter 6.*

Prostitution

Is prostitution legal in France?

Yes. Prostitution is legal in France, but it is regulated by laws that aim to control aspects surrounding it. While selling sex is not illegal, soliciting (proactively offering sexual services in public) is prohibited, and certain practices related to prostitution, such as pimping and human trafficking, are strictly illegal. *For more details, see Chapter 7.*

LGBTQ

Is homosexuality legal in France?

Yes. Homosexuality is legal in France. The country decriminalized homosexuality in 1791, and same-sex relationships have been fully accepted in law.

Are same sex public displays of affection legal?

Yes. PDA is legal in France. There are no specific laws prohibiting same-sex couples from publicly expressing affection, and France is generally considered to be tolerant and supportive of LGBTQ+ rights. In fact, same-sex marriage has been legal in France since 2013, and the country has anti-discrimination laws that protect LGBTQ+ individuals in various aspects of life, including employment and public spaces. *For more details, see Chapter 8.*

Arrested in France

Would I be entitled to bail if I'm arrested?

If you're arrested in France, whether you are entitled to bail depends on the nature of the crime and the circumstances surrounding your arrest. For most minor offenses, you may be released on bail or under judicial supervision while awaiting trial. However, for serious crimes or if you are considered a flight risk, bail might not be granted, and you could remain in pre-trial detention. The decision is ultimately made by the investigating judge or the prosecutor.

Will a lawyer be provided to me if I cannot afford one?

Yes. If you cannot afford a lawyer, France guarantees the right to legal representation for those unable to pay. If you are arrested or face serious charges, a lawyer will be appointed to you by the state, regardless of your financial situation. This is part of France's commitment to ensuring fair trials and legal protections for all individuals, as required by the European Convention on Human Rights. *For more details, see Chapter 10.*

Helping a Friend or Relative Imprisoned in France

Can I send money to a friend or relative imprisoned in France?

Yes, you can send money to a person in prison in France, typically through a prison account or authorized services. The funds can be used for personal expenses like food, toiletries, or phone cards. You should check with the specific prison for their procedures.

Can I remain in France upon release from prison or jail after my sentence is complete?

If you're an EU citizen or legal resident, you can generally stay in France after serving your sentence. However, non-EU nationals may face deportation, especially for serious crimes. It's best to consult an immigration lawyer for specific advice. *For more details, see Chapter 12.*

Crime Victim Assistance

Can a victim of a crime be legally compensated?

Yes. Victims of crime in France can be legally compensated. The French legal system provides compensation for victims of violent crimes, including assault, robbery, and sexual offenses. Victims can seek compensation through the courts or by applying for financial assistance from the National Fund for Compensation of Victims of Crime (*Fonds de Garantie des Victimes*). This fund provides compensation for victims who are unable to obtain restitution from the offender.

Does the French government offer assistance for family members of homicide victims?

Yes. The French government does aid family members of homicide victims. They may be eligible for financial support, counseling, and other services. This assistance is provided by both state-funded programs and victim support organizations. In addition, family members can apply for compensation through the *National Fund for Compensation of Victims of Crime*, which covers medical expenses, funeral costs, and other related expenses. *For more details, see Chapter 14.*

Police

Is there an official police force?

Yes. France has an official police force with two main agencies: the Police Nationale, responsible for urban areas and general law enforcement, and the Gendarmerie Nationale, which operates mainly in rural areas and handles military-style policing and highway patrol. Both forces work together to maintain public safety. *For more details, see Chapter 15.*

How to Get Legal Help in France

Is there a resource in France to find legal representation?

Yes. When visiting France, there are several resources available for legal representation. The *Paris Bar Association* offers pro bono services and can connect individuals with lawyers for various legal issues, including immigration and criminal matters. Additionally, organizations like *Les Points d'accès au Droit* provide free consultations across Paris, addressing everyday legal issues such as employment and family law. Visitors may also seek assistance from Houses of Justice and Law, which are managed by the Ministry of Justice. Home embassy or consulate is also a great resource to provide you with information on local attorneys.

Is there free legal representation assistance?

Yes, free legal representation is available in France through legal aid (*aide juridictionnelle*). This assistance is provided to individuals who cannot afford to pay for a lawyer. Eligibility is based on income and financial resources, and you can apply for legal aid through the local court or legal aid office. If granted, it can cover all or part of the cost of your legal representation. *For more details, see Chapter 16.*

Foreign Embassies in France

Are there foreign embassies in France?

Yes, there are numerous foreign embassies in France, particularly in Paris, where most countries have diplomatic missions. These embassies provide consular services, including assistance with emergencies, visas, and legal issues for their citizens living or traveling in France.

Is there a website to locate embassies in France?

Yes. To locate foreign embassies in France, you can visit the official French Ministry of Europe and Foreign Affairs website or use **EmbassyPages.com**, which has a comprehensive list of embassies and consulates in France. Additionally, many embassies have their own websites where you can find contact information and specific services they offer. *For more details, see Chapter 16.*

Medical Facilities & Hospitals

Is there a number I can call for ambulance and fire emergencies?

Yes. For ambulance or fire emergencies in France, you can call **112**, which is the European Union emergency number and works for police, fire, and medical emergencies. Alternatively, you can also call **15**

for medical emergencies (ambulance), and **18** for fire emergencies. Both numbers are available 24/7.

If I am injured while on vacation in France, are there hospitals that are recommended for tourists?

Yes. If you are injured while on vacation in France, most major cities and tourist areas have public hospitals that handle emergencies. In Paris, *Hôpital Européen Georges-Pompidou* and *Hôpital Saint-Antoine* are well-regarded. In Nice, *CHU de Nice* is a major hospital, and in Marseille, *Hôpital de la Timone* is one of the largest and most recognized. These hospitals provide emergency care and can assist tourists, although it's advisable to have travel insurance to cover medical expenses. If needed, your embassy or local tourism office can help guide you to nearby medical facilities. *For more details, see Chapter 17.*

Driving in France

Which side of the road do I drive on?

In France, you drive on the right-hand side of the road.

Can I use my driver's license from my home country to drive in France?

Yes. You can use your driver's license from your home country to drive in France for up to one year if you are a tourist. However, if you are planning to stay longer or are a resident, you may need to exchange your foreign license for a French one, depending on your country of origin.

How old do I need to be to rent a car?

To rent a car in France, you generally need to be at least 21 years old, though this can vary by rental agency. Drivers under 25 may also face an additional young driver surcharge, and some rental companies may have higher age restrictions for certain vehicle categories. *For more details, see Chapter 18.*

Nude Beaches & Clothing-Optional Resorts

Is public nudity legal on the beaches?

In France, public nudity on beaches is legal, but it is regulated. There are designated nudist beaches (*plages naturistes*) where nudity is allowed and socially accepted. These beaches are clearly marked and typically located in more secluded or rural areas. However, on non-designated public beaches, nudity is generally not permitted, and you could be fined for indecent exposure. Always check for signs indicating whether nudity is allowed or appropriate in a specific area. *For more details, see Chapter 19.*

Tourist Taxation

Is there a room tax in France?

Yes, there is an accommodation tax in France, known as the *taxe de séjour*. This tax is applied to tourists staying in hotels, vacation rentals, campsites, and other forms of accommodation. The amount varies depending on the location, the type of accommodation, and its rating (e.g., star rating for hotels). This tax is typically paid per person, per night, and is collected by the accommodation provider.

Is there any fee associated with leaving France?

No. There is no fee associated with leaving France. However, if you are flying internationally, there may be airport taxes or departure taxes included in the cost of your flight ticket, but these are generally included in the overall fare, not paid separately when leaving the country. Additionally, if you are traveling from an overseas territory (like Guadeloupe or Réunion), there may be additional specific taxes. *For more details, see Chapter 22.*

Long-Term Stays

Do I need to return to my home country to apply for a work permit in France?

> **Yes.** If you're a non-EU citizen, you generally need to apply for a work permit in your home country or a country where you have legal residence. The process starts with a job offer from a French employer, who will apply for the permit. In some cases, you may be able to apply for a work permit while in France, but it's more complicated and depends on your visa type. Always check with the French consulate for specific details.

As an American, how long can I stay in France without a visa?

> As an American citizen, you can stay in France for up to 90 days within a 180-day period without a visa, under the Schengen Area agreement. This applies to tourism, business trips, or family visits. If you wish to stay longer than 90 days, you will need to apply for a long-stay visa or a residence permit depending on the purpose of your stay (e.g., work, study, or family reunification). *For more details, see Chapter 23.*

In the Event of Death

What documents would an embassy need regarding the death of a tourist?

> If a tourist dies in France, the embassy will need the death certificate, the passport or identification, and a medical report (if applicable). They will also require contact information for the next of kin, a formal request for assistance, and details of any travel insurance. The embassy can help with repatriation, funeral arrangements, and legal processes, but the family will need to coordinate with local authorities and funeral homes. *For more details, see Chapter 25.*

U.S. Consulate Assistance

Are there any limitations to the consulate assistance I can receive while in France?

Yes. Consulates in France can assist with emergency situations but have limitations. They cannot provide financial support, cover legal fees, or intervene in legal matters like criminal cases unless there's unlawful detention. They also can't bypass French laws or share information without your consent due to privacy regulations. *For more details, see Chapter 14.*

EMERGENCY/IMPORTANT CONTACT NUMBERS IN FRANCE

 Please consider putting some of these numbers in your phone prior to traveling to France.

EMERGENCY NUMBERS

- **EMERGENCY SERVICES (POLICE, FIRE, AMBULANCE): 112**

  This is the universal European emergency number and can be dialed free of charge from any phone, including mobile phones.

- **POLICE EMERGENCY (FOR IMMEDIATE DANGER): 17**

- **FIRE BRIGADE (FOR FIRE-RELATED EMERGENCIES OR ACCIDENTS): 18**

- **AMBULANCE/MEDICAL EMERGENCIES (SAMU): 15**

SPECIALIZED NUMBERS

- **MARITIME RESCUE: 196**

  For emergencies at sea.

- **EMERGENCY FOR THE HEARING IMPAIRED: 114**

  Accessible via SMS or fax for those who are deaf or hard of hearing.

NON-EMERGENCY NUMBERS

- MEDICAL ASSISTANCE (NON-URGENT): 116 117
  For minor injuries or to consult a doctor.

- TOURIST HELPLINE (FRANCE): +33 1 70 18 95 29
  Assistance for visitors, available in multiple languages.

- LOST OR STOLEN CREDIT CARDS:
  Visa: +33 4 42 60 53 03
  Mastercard: +33 1 42 77 78 03

- SOS DOCTORS (HOME VISITS): 36 24

OTHER USEFUL NUMBERS

- PHARMACY ON-CALL (DRUGSTORE LOCATOR): 3237
- TRANSPORTATION (TAXI G7): 3607

USEFUL FRENCH PHRASES

Greetings

HI/HELLO – Bonjour

GOOD MORNING – Bonjour

GOOD AFTERNOON – Bon après-midi

GOOD NIGHT – Bonne nuit

GOODBYE – Au revoir

Magic Words

PLEASE – S'il vous plaît

THANK YOU – Merci

YOU'RE WELCOME – De rien

CHEERS! – Santé !

EXCUSE ME – Excusez-moi

Getting Around

WHERE IS THE BATHROOM? – Où sont les toilettes ?

WHAT TIME IS IT? – Quelle heure est-il ?

HOW DO I GET TO...? – Comment puis-je aller à... ?

WHERE DOES THIS TRAIN/BUS GO? – Où va ce train/bus ?

RESTAURANT – Restaurant

HOW MUCH DOES THIS COST? – Combien cela coûte-t-il ?

TRAIN/METRO STATION – Gare/station de metro

Communication

DO YOU SPEAK ENGLISH? – Parlez-vous anglais ?

I DO NOT UNDERSTAND – Je ne comprends pas

I DON'T SPEAK FRENCH – Je ne parle pas français

I DON'T KNOW – Je ne sais pas

Emergency

HELP! – À l'aide !

CALL AN AMBULANCE! – Appelez une ambulance !

I NEED A DOCTOR – J'ai besoin d'un médecin

POLICE – Police

I'M LOST – Je suis perdu(e)

IT'S AN EMERGENCY – C'est une urgence

GLOSSARY

ACQUITTAL: A jury verdict that a criminal defendant is not guilty, or the finding of a judge that the evidence cannot support a conviction.

ADVERSARY PROCEEDING: A lawsuit arising from a controversy that begins with filing a complaint.

AFFIDAVIT: A written statement made under oath.

APPEAL: A request made after a trial court has decided against one party in which the losing party asks a higher court to review the decision for legal error.

ARRAIGNMENT: A proceeding in which a criminal defendant is brought to court, told of the charges, and asked to plead guilty or not guilty.

BAIL: The temporary release of a person from jail when awaiting trial, on condition that a sum of money be lodged or deposited to guarantee an appearance in court.

BARRISTER: A lawyer admitted to plead at the Bar and who may try cases in superior court.

BURDEN OF PROOF: The duty to prove disputed facts.

CAUSE OF ACTION: A legal claim in a civil action.

COMPLAINT: A written statement that begins a civil lawsuit in which the plaintiff details the claims.

CONTRACT: An agreement between two or more persons to do something or to not do something.

CONVICTION: A judgment of guilt against a person charged with a crime.

CUSTOMS DUTY: A tariff or tax imposed on goods when transported across international borders.

COURT LIAISON: A person that coordinates with attorneys to perform administrative duties, such as scheduling witnesses, sharing information with law enforcement, and overseeing the reporting of cases to foreign embassies when applicable.

DAMAGES: Money that a defendant pays to a plaintiff in a civil case if the plaintiff wins.

DEFENDANT: 1) The individual against whom a civil claim is filed; 2) The individual against whom a criminal charge is filed.

FELONY: A serious crime, punishable by more than one year in prison.

MAGISTRATE: A judicial officer of a district court, who conducts initial proceedings in criminal cases, decides criminal misdemeanor cases, conducts many pretrial civil and criminal matters on behalf of district judges, and decides civil cases with the consent of the parties.

MISDEMEANOR: An offense punishable by one year or less in jail.

PLAINTIFF: A person or business that files a formal complaint with the court.

PLEA: In a criminal case, the answer of "guilty," "not guilty," or "no contest" in response to a criminal charge.

SOLICITOR: A lawyer who advises clients, represents them in lower court, and prepares cases for barristers to try in higher courts.

SOVEREIGN IMMUNITY: A legal doctrine by which the sovereign or the state (i.e. government) cannot commit a legal wrong and thus, it is immune from criminal and civil liability and cannot be sued.

STATUTE: A written law passed by a legislative body.

STATUTE OF LIMITATIONS: A statute prescribing a period of limitation to bring certain types of legal actions. If the action is not brought within that time, the person or entity (in a criminal context) is permanently barred from suing in court.

SUBPOENA: A command, issued under court authority, for a witness to appear and to give testimony.

TESTIMONY: Evidence presented orally by witnesses.

VERDICT: The decision of a judge or jury in a case.

WARRANT: Court authorization to conduct a search or to make an arrest.

ACKNOWLEDGMENTS

This book series would never have seen the light of day without the able assistance of the following people:

Kathy Adams, my paralegal for over 22 years, who is the "Best" I've ever worked with during my entire legal career because of her amazing work ethic, organizational skills, and her ability to think outside of the box in unique and creative ways;

Ally Knez-Siddique, a professional writer, and one of my paralegals, whose eye for detail, according to her, is both a blessing and a curse;

Gino Ibanez, my former law clerk, whose exceptional research skills helped move this book series along in its early stages;

Rosa Diaz Graham, my legal assistant who helped with research and word processing at the very beginning of this project;

Shelia Martin, one of my former paralegals, worked diligently on this series of books, even after taking on another job. Her organizational skills are reflected throughout;

Mindy Scarlett, my marketing and publishing "Guru"! Her creativity and vision have no boundaries!

ABOUT THE AUTHOR

Michael L. Moore practices in Orlando, Florida, the city where he spent his formative years. He credits the trauma of having his brother murdered when he was only 10 years old, as the catalyst that drew him into the practice of law.

Moore attended Florida State University, where he was a member of the FSU debate team. Upon graduating, he was awarded a full scholarship to attend the University of Tennessee College of Law, where he was elected President of the Student Bar Association. He further honed his advocacy and public speaking skills by participating in 'moot court' competitions.

After clerking at the Tennessee Attorney General's office while in law school, Moore moved back to Orlando, Florida, to work at the State Attorney's Office as a prosecutor, and where he was fortunate enough to meet the young lady that would eventually become his wife. Moore moved on to working for private law firms, both local and national, and eventually established his own law firm in 1999. He continues to make Orlando his home base.

It was the murder of a close friend and client in Jamaica that caused Moore to realize that books on laws in other countries were few and far between, and he was inspired to create Law of the Land Publishing. Moore launched Law of the Land Publishing to provide a series of guidebooks and a membership site for tourists and business travelers to stay up to date on the laws in each country they travel to, as well as having access to assistance if they run into legal issues.

"My vision is to educate people on what their legal rights are, and how they can access legal assistance, no matter where they have to travel to in the world," said Moore. "As Americans, we have a right to due process, but in some countries, you don't even have the right to access a square meal when incarcerated. My goal is to provide the information needed to stay out of trouble, as well as having access to assistance if trouble finds you."

www.ingramcontent.com/pod-product-compliance
Lightning Source LLC
Chambersburg PA
CBHW051136120626
46547CB00012B/829